LOOKING BACK
BY
JOHN HINSEY

PROLOGUE

"LOOKING BACK" TELLS HOW EVENTS BROUGHT ABOUT MASSIVE CHANGES THROUGHOUT MY LIFE OF NINETY-FIVE YEARS. I FELT COMPELLED TO CHRONICLE THAT THOSE DRAMATIC MOMENTS HAD TURNED ME INTO A DIFFERENT PERSON WITH A NEW DIRCECTION, NEW OBJECTIVES AND A NEW, MORE SUITABLE LIFESTYLE AN AMAZING, AT LAST COUNT, I BELIEVE, NINE TIMES.

I AM VERY GRATEFUL FOR HAVING HAD SUCH A STRANGE AND EXCITING LIFE. IT HAS HAD ME REACH THE HIGHEST POSSIBLE LEVEL OF LOYALITY AND LOVE FOR OURSELVES, FOR OUR WORLD AND ALL THAT SURROUNDS US.

CHAPTER

1

I WAS BORN IN A CITY NAMED BOONE IN THE CORN GROWING STATE OF IOWA ON MAY 12, 1921. MY FATHER, HERBERT HINSEY, AND MY MOTHER, RUTH HINSEY, WERE QUINTESSENTIAL MIDWESTENERS LIVING IN AN EXEMPLARY MIDWESTERN TOWN WITH ABOUT 12,000 TRUE TO TYPE MIDWESTERN RESIDENTS. IT WAS A NEAT FRONT YARD COMMUNITY THAT BOASTED HAVING A JCPENNY'S, AN EARLY MOTION PICTURE THEATER, AND CONVENIENT NEIGHBORHOOD GROCERY STORES. IT WAS ALSO A STOP-OVER FOR THE CHICAGO NORTH WESTERN RAILROAD. MY FATHER WORKED FOR THE RAILROAD. MY MOTHER WAS A HOUSEWIFE. SHE WAS SURROUNDED BY A LARGE FAMILY AND LONG-STANDING FRIENDS FOR SHE TOO WAS BORN IN BOONE.

THEY LIVED IN A SMALL HOUSE THAT MY FATHER HAD BUILT ON THE CITY'S OUTSKIRTS. IN ALL LIKELYHOOD, IT WAS A PLEASANT LIFE UNTIL I BARGED INTO IT WEIGHING OVER THIRTEEN POUNDS. THAT SUPERABUNDANCE OF POUNDAGE TURNED WHAT SHOULD HAVE BEEN A JOYFUL OCCASION TO ONE OF REJECTION. MY MOTHER NEVER FORGAVE ME FOR THE HOURS OF EXCRUTIATING PAIN SHE HAD TO ENDURE WHILE BEARING AND BIRTHING ME. HER FEELINGS OF ANGER AND BITTERNESS WERE UNCEASING THROUGH OUT MY EARLY YEARS. SHE WAS INDIFFERENT TO MY WELFARE, IMPATIENT AND UNYIELDING IN HER DISLIKE OR DISAPROVAL OF WHATEVER I HAD DONE OR WAS DOING. I WAS NOT PHYSICALLY ABUSED, BUT MY BODY OR MIND WILL NEVER BE FULLY CLEAN OF HER. SHE COULD HAVE PERMENENTLY DAMAGED A YOUNG LIFE. FORTUNATELY, I WAS GIANT STEPS FROM BEING FOREVER RESTRICTED OR OBLITERATED BECAUSE OF THE CALMING PRESENCE OF MY FATHER. HE WAS THE CENTER OF MY TINY WORLD.

THE ONLY TIME I REMEMBER HER BEING A TRUE "MOM" WAS WHEN SHE TAUGHT ME HOW TO TIE MY SHOES. THERE MUST HAVE BEEN MORE THAN ONE WAY, BUT SHE CHOSE A METHOD THAT HAD THE LACES LOOSEN EASILY. I WAS A GRACELSS KID WHO WAS DANGEROUSLY PIGEON-TOED. WHEN THE LACES WERE TANGLED WITH MY LUCKLESS FEET I WOULD FALL. IN THE SUMMER, I HAD UNINTERRUPTED CRUSTED KNEES WHICH SHE DIDN'T SEEM TO NOTICE. IN THE WINTER, SHE WAS KEENLY AWARE AND WILDLY UPSET BY MY ALMOST DAILY TOPPLINGS WHEN THEY MEANT ANOTHER PATCH JOB ON PANTS ALREADY HEAVY WITH THICK STICHES.

AS AN ADULT, LOOSE SHOE LACES ARE A POTENTIAL FOR BROKEN BONES AND A LONG HOSPITAL STAY. THEY ARE, HOWEVER, ALSO REMINDERS OF THE ONE AND ONLY TIME MY MOTHER WAS A MOM, SO I STILL TIE UP MY REEBOKS HER WAY TO KEEP THE MEMORY.

I WAS SEVEN WHEN DAD CAME HOME EARLY TO PROUDLY ANNOUNCE THAT HE HAD BEEN ELEVATED TO SUPERVISOR AND WAS BEING TRANSFERRED TO CHICAGO. I COULD SEE THAT MY MOTHER WAS NOT PLEASED. I REMEMBER HER SAYING SOMETHING, SHE DID NOT YELL AT DAD AS SHE DID AT ME, THAT IMPLIED CLEARLY THAT SHE DIDN'T THINK A NEW TITLE AND A RAISE IN PAY WAS WORTH BEING SEPERATED FROM FAMILY AND FRIENDS.

THREE WEEKS LATER, THOUGH OBVIOUSLY VERY UNHAPPY, MY MOTHER PACKED OUR SUITCASES AND WE JOINED MY FATHER IN THE CITY FAMOUS FOR ITS SIZE, SMELLY STOCKYARDS, HIGH WINDS AND LIVELY JAZZ. FROM THE FIRST DAY ON, SHE MADE MANIFEST HER HATRED FOR THE BIG, BURLY CITY. HER LOATHING INCREASED WHEN CHICAGO WAS HIT HARD BY THE GREAT DEPRESSION THAT FOLLOWED THE STOCK MARKET CRASH ON OCTOBER 29, 1929. A YEAR AFTER THAT MILESTONE DATE I CAME HOME FROM SCHOOL TO FIND THAT MY MOTHER WAS GONE ALONG WITH ALL OF HER CLOTHES. SHE HAD LEFT US, BUT IT WASN'T DIFFICULT FOR MY FATHER TO FIND HER. SHE WAS BACK HOME WITH HER PARENTS IN BOONE. HE CALLED AND TALKED TO HER NUMEROUS TIMES. I HEARD HIM OFFER TO COME BACK TO BOONE BUT SHE APPARENTLY WAS ADAMENT IN WANTING A DIVORCE. HE FINALLY STOPPED CALLING AND DIVORCE PROCEEDINGS BEGAN.

CHAPTER

2

MY FATHER'S PROMOTION BROUGHT US TO CHICAGO AND MASSIVE CHANGES THAT SUITED HIM BUT NOT MY MOTHER. IN THE 1920'S, CHICAGO'S BUSINESS DISTRICT, CALLED THE LOOP, HAD THEATERS, UNLIMITED SHOPPING, A GIANT PARK, CLANGING STREET CARS, BUSTLING TRAFFIC AND ABOVE ALL THAT THE ELEVATED TRAINS RAN UNMOLESTED. THE CITY EPITOMIZED THE ROMANTIC ERA OF PROHIBITION, FLAPPERS, JAZZ AND GANGSTERS WHICH WAS STIMULATING AND EXCITING FOR SOME BUT NOT FOR MRS. RUTH HINSEY.

BOONE'S BUSINESS DISTRICT WAS MAYBE TWO BLOCKS LONG WITHOUT, AS I REMEMBER, EVEN ONE TWO-STORY BUILDING. MY MOTHER WALKED TO WHERE EVER SHE WANTED TO GO AND KNEW AND GREETED ALMOST EVERYBODY SHE PASSED. HER FUN LOVING BROTHERS, BUNNY AND FARR, HER SISTER, MARIE, HER HUSBAND AND "LITTLE DEAN," NAMED AFTER HIS GRANDPA, DEAN BRICKER, WERE THERE TO COMFORT HER.

THE PROMOTION THAT BROUGHT MY MOTHER TO EXPERIENCE A BIG CITY'S INVIRONMENT COULD HAVE CHANGED THE COURSE OF HER LIFE, BUT JUST BECAUSE THERE'S A LIFE-ALTERING EVENT DOESN'T MEAN IT'S ALWAYS FOR THE BETTER. SHE COULDN'T OR WOULDN'T BECOME SOMEONE SHE WASN'T. SHE CHOSE TO REGAIN CONTROL OVER HER LIFE BY LEAVING HER HUSBAND AND SON BEHIND AND GO BACK TO WHERE SHE WAS RELEVANT AND CONTENT. I THINK MY MOTHER DID THE RIGHT THIING BY STAYING A SMALL TOWN WOMAN, THERE WERE FEWER DEMANDS MADE OF HER.

THEN, I MISSED NOT HAVING A MOTHER AND PROBABLY MISSED HER MORE THAN I LET ON. TODAY, I HOPE THAT UPON HER RETURN TO HER FAMILY SHE WAS AT PEACE AND FOUND SOMEONE TO LOVE. AND WHEN SHE HAD HER FINAL DIVORCE DECREE THEY MARRIED AND LIVED CHILDLESS IN A VERY NICE HOUSE WITH A VERY NICE WHITE PICKET FENCE. THAT IS A DAYDREAM, OF COURSE. ACTUALLY I KNOW NOTHING OF HER LIFE FOLLOWING THE DIVORCE, THERE WERE NO PHONE CALLS, CHRISTMAS CARDS, LETTERS, BIRTHDAY GREETINGS OR WEEKEND VISITS.

NOTHING CATASTROPHIC HAPPENED TO ME AFTER I WAS TOLD THAT MY MOTHER WAS NEVER COMIMG BACK. HER REPUDIATION OF ME IN MY FORMATIVE YEARS DID CAUSE ME TO SEEK APPROVAL FROM OTHERS. I WANTED DESPERATELY TO BE LIKED. THERE WAS SOMETHING LONGING IN THE WAY I WOULD APPROACH SOMEONE NEW IN AN EARNEST WAY TO MAKE A NEW FRIEND. I REMEMBER MY FATHER OFFERED NO SOOTHING PLATITUDES LIKE, "DON'T YOU WORRY, EVERYTHING WILL BE ALL RIGHT." SOMEHOW, HE MADE ME, A NINE YEAR KID, FEEL THE SAME AS IF SHE HAD DIED AND WAS IN A HAPPIER PLACE. I KNEW ABOUT PEOPLE DYING AND THAT THEY COULD NEVER RETURN OR BE BLAMED FOR LEAVING. SO, BEING LEFT BEHIND WASN'T AS ONEROUS AS IT COULD HAVE BEEN. I WAS TOLD

YEARS LATER THAT THERE WAS A STIPULATION IN THE DIVORCE DECREEE THAT I WAS TO LIVE WITH MY FATHER. EVEN THAT DIDN'T BOTHER ME.

HER "DYING" MEANT THAT A FATHER AND HIS YOUNG SON HAD TO MAKE A LIFE JUST FOR TWO AND NOT THE USUAL THREE. IT WASN'T AN UNCONVENTIONAL ARRANGEMENT IN THE NINETEEN THIRTIES. THE GREAT DEPRESSION ADDED TO A DENSE THICKET OF POTENTIAL PROBLEMS THAT WE HAD TO WORK THROUGH. CHICAGO THEN WAS A DANGEROUS PLACE AND COMBINED WITH THE ECOMOMIC CRISIS EVEN MORE TRECHEROUS. I, HOWEVER, ADOPTED A TOUGH GUY ATTITUDE TO SURVIVE. DAD THOUGHT FOR A WHILE THAT THE DEPRESSION WOULD COST HIM HIS JOB AT THE RAIROAD. THAT WAS SCARY. THEY DIDN'T FIRE HIM, BUT THEY DID CUT HIS SALARY SEVERLY. WE HAD ENOUGH FOR THE ESSENTIALS, SHELTER, FOOD AND CLOTHES ADEQUATE TO GET THROUGH EACH PITILESS CHICAGO WINTER, BUT NOT MUCH MORE.

SINCE IT WAS ONLY THE TWO OF US, WE MOVED INTO A ONE BEDROOM APARTMENT IN AN AREA ON THE FAR WESTSIDE OF CHICAGO CALLED AUSTIN. HE SLEPT ON A PULLOUT BED IN THE LIVING ROOM. I HAD THE BEDROOM WITH A DESK FOR SCHOOL WORK. EVERY AFTERNOON AFTER SCHOOL, I DELIVERED GROCERIES FOR A LOCAL MARKET FROM THREE TO SIX AND ON SATURDAY FROM EIGHT TO SIX. (I MADE ONLY THREE DOLLARS A WEEK, BUT IT HELPED.) WITH HOMEWORK FINISHED, OUR EVENINGS WERE COMPANIONABLE SITTING SIDE BY SIDE LISTENING TO THE RADIO. SOMETIMES I'D CRAWL UP IN HIS LAP AND FALL ASLEEP. HE GAVE ME WHAT WAS MISSING, THE SOFTER ASPECTS OF FAMILY.

CHAPTER

3

MOVIES HAD BEEN ONE OF MY FAVORITE RECREATONS AS A TEENAGER. MOVIE THEATERS WERE COMFORTING. EVERY SUNDAY, I COULD BE FOUND IN ONE OR TWO OF THE MOVIE THEATRES WITHIN WALKING DISTANCE OF OUR APARTMENT. A TICKET TO SEE A MOVIE COST TEN CENTS. OCCASIONALLY, WHEN I WENT TO TWO THEATRES IT COST ME TWENTY CENTS OF MY HARD EARNED MONEY. NICKLES AND DIMES DURING THE DEPRESSION WERE JUDICIOUSLY SPENT.

ONE SUNDAY DAD AND I WENT BY STREETCAR TO THE BEAUTIFUL, FIRST- RUN THEATRE ON BELMONT AVENUE TO SEE FRANK BUCK'S "BRING 'EM BACK ALIVE," A FILM SHOT IN AFRICA. IT WAS HIS TREAT. THE STREETCAR RIDE WAS SEVEN CENTS FOR DAD AND THREE CENTS FOR ME. THE THEATRE TICKETS COST A TOTAL OF THIRTY-FIVE CENTS. AFTER THE MOVIE, WE RODE THE STREETCAR BACK TO AUSTIN, AND WENT TO AN EATERY THAT SOLD SMALL BUT DELICIOUS HAMBURGERS FOR A NICKLE A PIECE. WE EACH HAD TWO. THE AFTERNOON'S "SQUANDERING" OF SEVENTY-FIVE CENTS WAS WORTH EVERY PENNY. WE HAD A SPECIAL DAY SEEING A GREAT MOTION PICTURE THAT GAVE US THE WILD ANIMALS OF AFRICA TO TALK ABOUT FOR MONTHS.

MY FATHER SEIZED EVERY OPPORTNITY TO HELP US LIVE IN FULL ACCORD. HE WAS A FABULOUS "DAD" AND I RESPECTED AND LOVED HIM AS A CHILD AND THEN AS A MAN.

EDITH JACKSON, A VERY PLEASANT WOMAN, CAME INTO HERBERT F. HINSEY'S LONELY LIFE AND THEY BECAME HUSBAND AND WIFE IN 1936. WE MOVED INTO A SLIGHTY LARGER APARTMENT ON JACKSON BOULEVARD. WE COULD AFFORD THE APARTMENT BECAUSE THE RAILROAD HAD ADDED PART OF DAD'S SALARY THEY'D TAKEN AWAY FROM HIS PAYCHECK.

IN 1935, I LOOKED FORWARD TO HIGH SCHOOL, BUT SOON FOUND IT JUST AS DULL AND UNINSPIRING AS GRAMMAR SCHOOL. MY TEENAGE YEARS AND MY TIME AT AUSTIN HIGH WERE LACKLUSTER. I SIMPLY EXISTED. I DIDN'T KNOW WHAT I WANTED TO DO OR BE AS AN ADULT, BUT I KNEW I WANTED TO BE BETTER PREPARED FOR WHAT EVER LIE AHEAD. I BECAME DETERMINED TO MOVE JUST NORTH OF CHICAGO TO EVANSTON AND ATTEND NORTWESTERN UNIVERSITY WHEN I GRADUATED FROM HIGH SCHOOL. GOING TO COLLEGE RIGHT AFTER HIGH SCHOOL WAS THE FIRST OF UNREALIZED SELF-FULFILLING GOALS.

THE DEPRESSION WAS WANING BUT UNEMPLOYMENT WAS STILL IN DOUBLE DIGITS IN 1940 WHEN I WAS ONE OF A THOUSAND YOUNG PEOPLE SAYING FAREWELL TO AUSTIN HIGH, THERE WERE NO FAMILY FUNDS TO SPARE AND NO COLLEGE. I GOT LUCKY AND FOUND AN AGREEABLE, BUT LOW PAYING, JOB. I WAS STUNNED TO LEARN ON SUNDAY, DECEMBER 7,1941. OF JAPAN'S SURPRISE ATTACKON OUR NAVAL BASE AT PEAR HARBOR, HAWAII. THE NEXT DAY PRESIDENT ROOSEVELT DECLARED WAR ON JAPAN. THAT DECLARATION WAS A MAJOR EVENT THAT DRASTICALLY CHANGED THE COURSE OF MY LIFE. INSTEAD OF STROLLING NORTHWESTERN'S CAMPAS, I WAS MARCHING

SMARTLY AROUND THE PARADE GROUNDS OF CAMP STEWART GEORGE FOLLOWING THE PORPOSFUL COMMANDS OF A TIRELESS SERGEANT.

THE WAR, THAT WAS TO END ALL WARS, BROUGHT UNCERTAINTY AS WELL AS AN OVERWHELMING SENSE OF DUTY TO COUNTRY. I RESENTED NOT GOING TO COLLEGE, BUT WENT UNCOMPLAINING TO MARCH AT CAMP STEWART IN GEORGIA INSTEAD OF STROLLING THE CAMPUS AT NORTHWESTERN.

AT CAMP STEWART, I NOT ONLY MARCHED, BUT HIKED, SALUTED A LOT, ATE TERRIBLE, LIFE-SUSTAINING FOOD, SOMETIMES SHOVED HEAVY SHELLS INTO REALLY BIG GUNS TO SIMULATE THE SHOOTING DOWN OF HOSTILE AIRCRAFT. IT WAS A HECTIC TIME GETTING YOUNG MEN READY TO TAKE ON AND DEFEAT OUR ENEMIES, BUT FEELING LETDOWN BECAUSE OF NOT BEING IN COLLEGE STILL LURKED IN THE BACK OF MY MIND.

ON A GLOOMY MORNING, OUR COMPANY MARCHED IN FORMATION TO THE FIRING RANGE. WHEN IT WAS MY TURN AT THE FIRING LINE, THE HEFT AND FEEL OF THE RIFLE THAT HELPED WIN THE WAR, THE M1, FELT GOOD. A SARGENT POINTED AT THE DISTANT BULL'S-EYE, AND SAID, "LINE IT UP USING THESE TWO SIGHTS," HE KINDLY POINTED THEM OUT, "AND SLOWLY SQUEEZE THE TRIGGER." I HAD NOTICED WHEN SOMEONE MISSED THE TARGET ENTIRELY A FLAG CALLED MAGGIE'S DRAWERS WAS WAVED. THERE WAS NO MAGGIE'S DRAWERS FOR ME. I, FROM EVERY POSITION, HIT THAT FAR OFF BLACK CIRCLE IN THE CENTER OF THE TARGET. AN EFFORT WAS MADE TO APPEAR NONCHALANT AS THE RIFLE WAS RETURNED TO THE SARGENT. HE WOULD NEVER KNOW THAT I'D HAD A 22 RIFLE TO SHOOT AT BOTTLES AND CANS FOR YEARS.

IT TURNED OUT TO BE QUITE A DAY, A REWARDING ONE. I WAS THE ONLY DRAFTEE TO SHOOT A PERFECT SCORE. A CAPTAIN CAME UP TO ME AS WE WERE LEAVING AND SAID I WAS TO REPORT TO HIM THE NEXT DAY TO HELP INSTRUCT. FOR THE FIRST TIME, A TOMORROW LOOKED PROMISING.

CHAPTER

4

RAIN WAS POURING DOWN WHEN I ARRIVED AT THE FIRING RANGE. THE CAPTAIN WAS SITTING UNDER THE OBSERVATION PLATFORM. HE CALLED ME OVER SAYING, "MAYBE IT WILL LET UP."

WE SAT AND TALKED FOR OVER TWO HOURS WHILE WATCHING THE SHEETS OF BLOWING RAIN. PART OF OUR CONVERSATION HAD TO DO WITH MY PREPARATION FOR COLLEGE AND NOT GOING BECAUSE OF THE WAR. THE RAIN DIDN'T STOP AND JUST BEFORE WE LEFT, HE ASKED IF I WOULD LIKE TO WORK FOR HIM AT BATTALION HEADQUARTERS. THE REJOINDER WAS THAT THAT WOULD BE GREAT, NOT KNOWING WHAT WAS ENTAILED, BUT KNEW IT WOULD BE DIFFERENT AND MAYBE MORE INTERESTING.

IN SHORT ORDER, I WAS SHUFFLING PAPERS FROM FILES TO DESKS AND BACK TO FILES. THE GOOD CAPTAIN CALLED ME OVER ONE AFTERNOON AND SAID, WITH A SMILE, "I'VE BEEN WATCHING THE WAY YOU CONDUCT YOURSELF AND I THINK YOU'RE OFFICER MATERIAL. I'M RECOMENDING YOU FOR OCS." SEEING MY TOTAL LACK OF COMPREHENSION, HE ADDED, "OFFICER'S CANDIDATE SCHOOL." THAT WAS CLEARLY AN UNEXPECTED' JAW-DROPPING SURPRISE. I WAS SPEECHLESS FOR A MOMENT, BUT RECOVERED BY THANKING THE CAPTAIN WITH PROPER MILITARY POSTURE.

UNBELIEVABLY, THREE DAYS LATER I WAS OFF TO CAMP DAVIS IN NORTH CAROLINA TO BECOME AN OFFICER AND A GENTLEMAN.

OCS WAS SOMETHING NO ONE COULD BE PREPARED FOR. IT WAS THREE MONTHS OF CHOROGRAPHED INTENT TO ENGENDER FEAR OF FAILURE. EVERY THURSDAY, APPROPRIATELY CALLED BLOODY THURSDAY, WE STOOD OUTSIDE THE BARRACKS, STARCH STIFF, AWAITING THE NAMES OF THOSE WHO HAD NOT MET THE SCHOOL'S OBSCURE STANDARDS.

IT WAS A JOLT SEEING SOME LEAVE, NOT TO BE SEEN AGAIN, AND NOT KNOWING WHAT THEY HAD DONE OR NOT DONE TO FAIL. THOSE APPALLING HUMILIATIONS MADE MOST, IF NOT ALL OF US WHO REMAINED DETERMINED TO PREVAIL.

I DON'T KNOW HOW I MADE IT THROUGH THE GRUELING, WRITTEN TESTS, ENDLESS PARADE GROUND DRILLS AND ALL THE BLOODY THURSDAYS, BUT I DID. ONLY TWENTY-ONE OF US AVOIDED BEING CALLED OUT ON ONE OF THOSE MERCILESS THURSDAYS.

PUTTING ON MY NEW UNIFORM WITH TWIN GOLD BARS, AND THEREBY HAVING THE RIGHT TO BE SALUTED, AND OBEYED IF I HAD AN ORDER HANDY, BROUGHT AN UNFAMILAR AND UNACCUSTOMED DIMENSION OF PRIDE TO MY LIFE THAT RESHAPED AND REDIRECTED ME FROM THAT DAY ONWARD. IT WAS AN EVENT THAT BROUGHT A NEW SELF-ASSURANCE, AND A NEW SUPPORTIVE SELF-IMAGE THAT

WOULD HELP ME MEET THE RESPONSIBILITIES OF AN OFFICER AND THE CHALLENGES OF AN UNCERTAIN FUTURE, THERE WAS NO CEREMONIAL GRADUATION, WE WERE SIMPLY HANDED ORDERS TELLING US WHERE TO REPORT FOR DUTY. MY ASSIGNMENT WAS TO CAMP HAAN IN SOUTHERN CALIFORNIA TO AWAIT ASSIGNMENT.

UPON ARRIVAL, I WENT ON A SELF-CONDUCTED TOUR OF THE CAMP AND RAN INTO SOMEONE I'D KNOWN SLIGHTLY AT OCS, ROGER DAVIS.

HE WAS A NATIVE CALIFORNIAN, BORN AND RAISED IN HOLLYWOOD. THE FOLLOWING WEEKEND I WENT WITH HIM TO WHERE ALL OF THOSE WONDERFUL MOVIES I SAW AND LOVED AS A KID WERE MADE. HIS FAMILY, HIS FIANCEE, NANCY, AND HER FRIEND, MILDRED KORNMAN, WHO HAD DROPPED BY TO SAY HELLO, WERE WELCOMING AND GRACIOUS. MILDRED WAS STUNNING. THE FOUR OF US DECIDED TO GO OUT TO DINNER AND WENT TO AN OUTSTANDING RESTAURANT CALLED "THE TAIL OF THE COCK" ON A BUSY STREET NAMED LA CIENEGA.

WE SAT AND TALKED ALMOST TO CLOSING. IT WAS REVEALED THAT MILDRED WAS UNDER CONTRACT TO TWENTITH CENTURY FOX AND AT THE STUDIO SHE WAS KNOWN AS RICKI VANDUSEN AND LIKED TO BE CALLED RICKI. THOUGH DELIVERED OFF HAND, IT WAS SLIGHTLY DISTRACTING TO LEARN THAT MY DINNER COMPANION WAS ACTUALLY A PART OF THE MOTION PICTURE BUSINESS. I DID NOT LET HER CLASSIC BEAUTY OR THAT SHE WAS UNDER CONTRACT TO A MAJOR STUDIO OVERWHEM ME. I WAS, HOWEVER, INORDINATELY PLEASED WHEN, AS WE WERE LEAVING THE RESTAURANT, SHE AGREED TO A LUNCH DATE THE NEXT DAY. HAVING VANQUISHED ALL OF THE EFFORTS OF OCS TO SEE ME FAIL AND NOT ACHIEVE THE DASHING UNIFORM OF AN OFFICER HAD ALREADY PAID OFF IN A HEAD SWELLING WAY.

ON MONDAY MORNING ROGER AND I MADE OUR WAY BACK TO CAMP HAAN'S POOL OF OFFICERS. WE WERE AT WAR WITH NOTHING TO DO BUT BIDE OUR TIME UNTIL SOMEONE OF AUTHORITY DECIDED WHAT TO DO WITH US. WEEKDAYS PASSED AT A SNAIL'S PACE. RICKI AND I HAD ESTABLISHED A RELATIONSHIP SO WEEKENDS WITH HER FLEW BY.

CHAPTER

5

RICKI WAS A PRIVILGED MEMBER OF A WELL ESTABLISHED HOLLYWOOD FAMILY. HER SISTER, MARY, HAD BEEN THE LOVEABLE LITLLE GIRL WITH CURLS OF OUR GANG COMEDIES. HER HUSBAND, RALPH MC CUTCHEON, RAISED AND TRAINED HORSES FOR THE MAJOR STUDIOS. GENE KORNMAN, RICKI'S FATHER, WAS KNOWN AS "THE PHOTOGRAHER OF STARS" AND HER STEPFATHER, LEE TRAVER, WAS THE CASTING DIRECTOR FOR AN ICON, SAMUEL GOLDWYN. OPPORTUNITIES TO LEARN MORE ABOUT THE INNER WORKINGS OF MOVIE MAKING WERE AMPLE AND ABSORBING.

FINALLY, AFTER TWO MONTHS, THERE WAS AN ORDER FOR ME TO REPORT TO THE TRANSPORTATION CORPS, A BRANCH OF THE ARMY IN SAN FRANCISCO THAT WAS RESPONSIBLE FOR TRANSPORTING PERSONNEL OR MATERIAL TO TROOPS IN COMBAT. UPON ARRIVAL, INSTEAD OF SPENDING THE NIGHT IN THE OFFICER'S QUARTERS, I CHOSE TO STAY AT ONE OF THE CITY'S WELL KNOWN HOTELS, WALK THE STREETS AND RIDE A CABLE CAR.

THAT DECISION MAY HAVE SAVED MY LIFE. ONE OF THE WOODEN BACHELOR QUARTERS CAUGHT FIRE AND BURNED TO THE GROUND KILLING MOST OF THE MEN SLEEPING INSIDE. SHAKEN BY THE NEWS OF THE POINTLESS DEATHS, THE NEXT DAY I REPORTED TO THE SHIP'S COMPLEMENT SECTION OCCUPYING ONE OF THE PIERS AT SAN FRANCISCO'S EMBARCADERO. THERE WAS A PALPABLE SADNESS THROUGH OUT THE SECTION'S OFFICES, BUT TIME WAS TAKEN TO EXLAIN THAT I WAS TO REPORT IN EVERY DAY BECAUSE I WOULD SOON BE ON A SHIP DELIVERING CARGO TO TROOPS SOMEWHERE IN THE SOUTH PACIFIC. I WAS GIVEN A DAILY PER DIEM FOR EXPENSES BEFORE BOARDING THE SHIP AND WAS DISMISSED.

THAT NIGHT I CALLED RICKI. WE BOTH AGREED THAT SPENDING THE NIGHT IN A HOTEL WAS A STROKE OF GOOD LUCK AND TALKING ABOUT IT SOMEHOW PUSHED US TOWARD A MORE SERIOUS RELATIONSHIP.

I MISSED HER THAT NIGHT AND CONTINUED TO MISS HER THROUGH OUT A LONG TRIP ON A FULLY LOADED SHIP TO A PLACE IN THE EAST INDIES CALLED NEW GUINEA. THE TRIP ACROSS THE PACIFIC OCEAN SEEMED TO LAST FOREVER. THE TRIP BACK TO SAN FRANCISCO SEEMED EVEN LONGER.

I HAD PARTICIPATED IN THE WAR THAT ENCOMPASSED, IN ONE WAY OR ANOTHER, THE WHOLE OF THE PLANET. THE SHIP WITH IT'S NEEDED SUPPLIES WAS NOT TORPEDOED, WE WERE NOT BOMBED OR SHOT AT WHILE UNLOADING, THERE WAS A CLEAN BED TO SLEEP IN EVERY NIGHT AND STILL THERE WAS A WARTIME SENSE OF UNPREDICTABILITY. I FACED A FUTURE THAT DIDN'T HAVE A CLEAR DESTINATION. MY CALLING RICKI AND PROPOSING MARRIAGE THAT FIRST NIGHT BACK WAS AN ATTEMPT TO ASSURE THAT THERE WAS A FUTURE. RICKI'S ACQUIESCENCE WAS A REFLECTION OF THE SAME WARTIME SENSIBILITIES. WISE OR NOT, WE WERE MARRIED A FEW DAYS LATER.

CHAPTER

6

MY CONTRIBUTION TO THE WAR EFFORT WAS NECESSARY, BUT TEDIOUSLY REPETITIVE UNTIL MY FINAL TRIP TO ALMOST THE OUTER LIMITS OF THE PACIFIC.

I BOARDED A NAVY LST, #799, A FLAT BOTTOMED VESSEL LOADED TO CAPACITY WITH AMMUNITION RANGING FROM EIGHT-INCH PHOSPHORUS TO FORTY-FIVE CALIBER SHELLS. ALL ANYONE KNEW AS WE MOVED CLUMSILY OUT UNDER THE GOLDENGATE BRIDGE WAS THAT WE WERE HEADED FOR HAWAII TO BECOME PART OF A HUGE CONVOY THAT WOULD TRAVEL AT OUR TOP SPEED OF SIX KNOTS.

I HAVE FORGOTTEN HOW LONG IT TOOK US TO ARRIVE THREE DAYS BEFORE THE INVASION OF OKINAWA TO JOIN THE LARGEST AMPHIBIOUS ASSULT IN THE PACIFIC WAR. WE WALLOWED IN NEARER THE BEACH AND MADE READY TO FUNCTION MUCH LIKE AN AMMUNITION DEPOT FOR THE INVADING TROOPS. AND TO LIVE THE ULTIMATE IN DARWINISM: SURVIVAL OF THE FITTEST. WHEN AT WAR IT IS REDUCED TO ITS REALISTIC CONCLUSION: KILL OR BE KILLED. THOSE OF US ON LST #799 WERE READY, HOWEVER, WE GOT LUCKY. THE RESISTENCE WAS FAR WEAKER THAN EXPECTED.

THE MOST EFFECTIVE OPPOSITION WAS FROM THE AIR. KAMIKAZE PILOTS FLEW IN AND TRIED TO PINPOINT INDIVIDUAL SHIPS IN DARING, SUICIDAL DIVES. STANDING ON THE DECK AWAITING THE LOUD WAILING SOUND WARNING OF ANOTHER KAMIKAZE ATTACK I LOOKED OUT AND WAS MOMENTARILY AWED BY THE SIGHT OF THE VAST ARRAY OF SHIPS, SOME CLOSE BY BUT THE REST FORMING AN IMPENETRABLE BLOCKAGE TO THE FAR-OFF HORIZON.   WHEN THE ALARM SOUNDED, AS EXPECTED, THE COMING ENEMY PLANE COUNT WAS GREATER THAN BEFORE. THE FIREPOWER COMING FROM ALL OF THOSE SHIPS WAS IMMENSE AND MOST OF THE UNARMED PLANES WERE LITERALLY TORN APART, BUT SOME PILOTS HIT THEIR TARGET WITH DEVASTATING EFFECT. ONE PASSED CLOSE ENOUGH SO THAT I COULD SEE THE PILOT SLUMPED OVER IN THE COCKPIT. 20 MM SHELLS FROM THE GUNS OF THE FARTHEST SHIPS FELL SHORT OF THEIR TARGETS AND EXPLODED ON OUR DECK.   THREE SAILORS SUFFERED LACERATED LEGS FROM SHRAPNEL FRAGMENTS. ONLY MINOR CASUALITIES WHEN BALANCED AGAINST THE VIOLENT ERUPTION WE WOULD HAVE CAUSED IF ONE OF THOSE DEAD PILOTS HAD AIMED HIS PLANE UNERRINGLY INTO OUR VULNERABLE LST.

AS THE TROOPS MOVED IN TO GAIN A BEACHHEAD WE STAYED CLOSE BEHIND. WHEN IN GOOD POSITION, WE DROPPED THE LST'S HUGE FRONT END AND TRIED TO TRANSFER NEEDED AMMUNITION TO THE SMALLER LCM'S - A CRAFT DESIGNED TO TRANSPORT CARGO AND/OR PERSONNEL FROM SHIP TO SHORE - BUT NOTHING WORKED AS PLANNED. THE RISE AND FALL OF THE OKINAWAN TIDE MADE A TRANSFER IMPOSSIBLE. WE PULLED BACK AND DAYS LATER RAN THE LST UP ON THE BEACH FOR A ROUTINE, BUT HIGHLY DANGEROUS UNLOADING.

THE SUICIDAL ATTACKS RELENLESSLY CONTINUED. WHEN THE WAILING SIREN ALERTED US, THE NAVY MANNED THEIR GUNS AND REST OF US WATCHED THE UNLOADING CREW RACE DOWN THE BEACH TO SAFETY. WHEN EMPTIED OF ALL THOSE EXPLOSIVES, EVERY MAN ABOARD TOOK A DEEP SIGH OF RELIEF.

WITH MY WRITTEN ORDERS, IN HAND, I SAID FAREWELL TO SHIP MATES, FOUND A NEWLY BULLDOZED AIR STRIP AND FLEW FROM ISLAND TO ISLAND TO HAWAII AND THEN ON TO SAN FRANCISCO. I ARRIVED MID MAY 1945, REPORTED IN AND WAS TOLD THAT I WAS NOW THE SECTION'S PERSONEL OFFICER FOR THE DURATION. I CALLED RICKI WITH THE GOOD NEWS AND MADE RESERVATIONS FOR TWO AT THE FAIRMONT HOTEL. MY COMING HOME TO STAY WAS TO BEGIN IN STYLE. RICKI ARRIVED THE NEXT DAY WITH SOME GOOD AND BAD NEWS. THE BAD WAS THAT FOX STUDIO HAD NOT RENEWED HER CONTRACT. THE GOOD WAS SHE COULD STAY PERMANENTLY IN SAN FRANCISCO. RICKI'S CONTRACT NOT BEING RENEWED DIDN'T CONCERN HER. SHE HAD NEVER THOUGHT OF HERSELF AS AN ACTRESS, BUT THE LOSS OF INCOME WOULD HURT.

GOOD FORTUNE COMES TO THOSE WHO HAVE A CONTENTED MIND, OR SOMETHING VERY SIMILAR TO IT WAS IN A NOVEL I'D READ RECENTLY PROBABLY BY P. D. JAMES OR JONATHAN KELLERMAN MY TWO FAVORITE AUTHORS. IT'S USE HERE IS TO MAKE CLEAR THAT IT WASN'T POSSIBLE FOR SOMEONE TO HAVE A MORE CONTENTED MIND THAN ME ON AUGUST I5, 1945, BECAUSE THAT IS THE DAY JAPAN SURRENDERED AND WORLD WAR 2 WAS FINALLY OVER. THE VERY BEST OF GOOD FORTUNE WAS, HOWEVER, MY BEING TOLD THAT RICKI WAS PREGNANT WITH OUR FIRST CHILD.

WHEN A WAR COMES TO AN END, YOU WOULD THINK THAT ONE WOULD BE DISCHARGED THE NEXT DAY. WELL, THAT'S NOT HOW THE ARMY DID WHAT IT HAD TO DO BY A WIDE MARGIN. THEY, WHOEVER THEY WERE, WAITED ROCKLIKE TO RELEASE ME FROM WHAT COULD BE REGARDED AS POINTLESS DUTIES. RICKI HAD GONE HOME TO HAVE THE BABY AND IT WAS THREE WEEKS AFTER STEPHEN SCOTT HINSEY'S BIRTH ON APRIL 2, 1946 THAT I WAS DISHARGD.

CHAPTER

7

RETURNING TO CIVILIAN LIFE BROUGHT A MYRIAD OF RESPONSIBILITIES TO BE SORTED OUT. I HAD DELT WITH RESPONSIBILITIES BEFORE SO I GEARED UP AND GOT ON WITH IT. A SERIES OF HAPPENINGS TOOK OVER.

ONE NIGHT, WHILE STROLLING ALONG VENTURA BOULEVARD IN STUDIO CITY, I SAW A WORKING TELEVISION SET IN A STORE WINDOW. I REMEMBER MY REACTION. I THOUGHT INSTANTLY THAT MOVING PICTURES COMBINED WITH SOUND WOULD SOON BE IN EVERY HOME. NOTHING COULD EVER REPLACE IT. TELEVISION WOULD DELIVER ANYTHING AND EVERYTHING IMAGINABLE TO ANYONE CAPABLE OF BUYING A BOXY THING WITH A SCREEN TO VIEW. IT WAS A HAPPENING THAT HAD ME FOCUS ON WHAT I WANTED TO DO, FIND A WAY TO BE A PART OF SOMETHING NEW AND EXCITING THAT OFFERED ENDLESS POSSIBILITIES. STRANGE HOW A GLANCE CAN BECOME THE FUTURE, BUT I NOW KNOW THAT A SINGLE MOMENT, SIMPLE AND DRAMATIC CAN CHANGE A LIFE FOREVER.

RICKI'S MOTHER, VERNA, A TYPICAL SHOW BIZ MOM, SAID ONE MORNING AT THE BREAKFAST TABLE, "YOU SHOULD BE AN ACTOR." SHE FOLLOWED THAT WITH, "I'LL MAKE A FEW CALLS."

I LIKED THE IDEA OF EARNING BIG BUCKS WHILE GAINING AN ENTRÉE INTO TELEVISION. BECOMING AN ACTOR, WITHOUT A HINT OF WHAT WAS REQUIRED TO BECOME ONE, WAS DAUNTING. NEVERTHELESS, VERNA'S CONVICTION THAT IT WAS THE RIGHT THING TO DO HELPPED ME GAIN THE COURAGE TO TRY. SHE WAS A GREAT HELP IN MAKING CONNECTIONS, KNOWING EVERYONE IN HOLLYWOOD OF NOTE.

THROUGH ONE CONNECTION, I WAS INTRODUCED TO FLORENCE ENRIGHT, THE WELL KNOWN HOLLYWOOD DRAMATIC COACH. SHE LOOKED ME OVER, ASKED ME TO READ SOMETHING FROM A SCRIPT, AND AFTER MY READING AGREED TO TAKE ME ON. MY PRIVATE SESSIONS WITH FLORENCE FOLLOWED JANE RUSSELL'S. I USED TO PASS HER ON THE STAIRWAY. WE WOULD EXCHANGE POLITE SALUTATIONS.

STIMULATING CLASSES AT UCLA AND SESSIONS AT THEATRE WORKSHOPS REINFORCED A GROWING RESOLVE. I WAS IN TWO PLAYS: ONE AT BLISS HAYDEN'S WORKSHOP, THE OTHER AT THE GELLER THEATRE. BENNY MEDFORD BECAME MY AGENT. HE WAS A DILIGENT, NO NONSENSE OLDER MAN WHO GOT ME IN TO READ FOR PRODUCERS AND CASTING PEOPLE AT ALL OF THE MAJOR STUDIOS. TRUTH IS THAT I WASN'T ADEQUATLY PREPARED FOR EVERTHING THAT WAS HAPPENING TO AND AROUND ME. NEVERTHELESS, UNIVERSAL WAS WILLING TO PUT ME UNDER CONTRACT, BUT THE STUDIO DELAYED THE SIGNING. THERE WAS A LOOMING JURISDICTIONAL STRIKE AND IF CALLED, WOULD SHUT DOWN ALL PRODUCTION THROUGHOUT THE INDUSTRY. THE STRIKE WAS CALLED AND WENT ON FOR DAYS WITH NO END IN SIGHT. IT WAS DIFFICULT TRYING TO FIND A DECENT PAYING JOB WHILE TRYING TO

BECOME AN ACTOR, BUT NOW IT WAS WORSE. THE STRIKE CAUSED ME AND THOUSANDS OF OTHERS SERIOUSLY GRAVE CONSEQUENCES.

I HAD JUST ENOUGH MONEY TO BUY A BUS TICKET TO CHICAGO WHERE I COULD STAY WITH MY FATHER AND STEPMOTHER, EDITH. I HOPED TO FIND WORK THERE AND COBBLE TOGETHER SUFFICIENT FUNDS TO GO ON TO NEW YORK AND TRY TO GAIN A FOOTHOLD IN THE THEATRE THERE. THAT WAS A DESPERATE SOLUTION, BUT AT THE TIME IT SEEMED VIABLE. RICKI AND STEPHEN MOVED TO HER MOTHER'S AND I, HEARTSICK BUT TRYING HARD TO LOOK AND ACT CONFIDENT, WAVED GOODBYE TO RICKI FROM A GREYHOUND BUS THAT LEFT THE BRIGHT SUNSHINE OF SOUTHERN CALIFORNA FOR A DREARY TRIP TO BLUSTRY CHICAGO.

ALL I WILL SAY ABOUT THE BUS TRIP WAS THAT IT WAS TORMENTINGLY LONG AND TORMENTINGLY MISERABLE. I ARRIVED IN CHICAGO EXHAUSTED. DAD AND EDITH WELCOMED ME WITH AN INVITATION TO FIRST SHOWER AND THEN TO GO TO MY OLD BEDROOM AND SATISFY MY OBVIOUS LONGING FOR A COMFORTABLE BED. IT WAS TWO DAYS BEFORE I HAD THE WILL OR THE ENERGY TO GO SEEKING A JOB AT THE CITY'S UNEMPLOYMENT OFFICE. THE PEOPLE THERE WERE EFFICIENTLY IMPERSONAL. WHEN I ASKED FOR ANY KIND OF WORK THAT PAID WELL, THE LADY DIDN'T EVEN LOOK AT ME, JUST WROTE DOWN AN ADDRESS TO A CEDAR FACTORY. I THOUGHT HOW APPROPRIATE WHEN I ARRIVED, BY SREET CAR, AT A LARGE, OPEN FLOORED BUILDING THAT SMELLED NICE AND MADE HOPE CHESTS.

I WAS HIRED WITHOUT A SINGLE QUESTION, JUST ASKED TO FILL OUT A FORM. FOR THREE MONTHS, I STOOD BEFORE A DRILL PRESS PUNCHING HOLES IN PIECES OF PRECUT CEDER, A WOOD OF THE PINE FAMILY THAT GIVES OFF THAT PLEASANT FRAGRANCE THAT WAS SO NOTICEABLE UPON ARRIVAL. I VOLUNTEERED FOR OVERTIME AT EVERY OPPORTNITY. I BOARDED WITH THE FOLKS GRATIS, EXCEPT FOR THE COST OF OCCASIONAL LITTLE THANK YOU GIFTS FOR EDITH AND FULL PAYMENT FOR MY SHORT CALLS TO RICKI AT NIGHT. DAD AND EDITH WERE GREAT, DIDN'T MAKE ME FEEL LIKE A MOOCHING HOUSE GUEST. I HOARDED MY EARNINGS, WANTING SUFFICENT CASH FOR THE UPCOMING STAY IN NEW YORK. I SAW AND TALKED TO OLD FRIENDS WHO WERE ALSO TRYING TO FIND THEIR WAY AFTER DICHARGES FROM THE MILITARY. WE HAD VERY LITTLE IN COMMON ANY MORE SO I SPENT MOST NIGHTS HABITUALLY LISTENING TO THE RADIO.

CHAPTER

8

A JOYIOUS GOODBYE TO MY DRILL PRESS, TO MY FOLKS AND CHICAGO PRECEDED A TRAIN RIDE, NO MORE BUSES, TO VISIT A FRIEND, LEROY BECKMAN AT CINCINNATI'S UNIVERSITY BEFORE GOING ON TO NEW YORK. LEROY WAS IN THE AIR FORCE. HE GOT SHOT DOWN OVER GERMANY, WAS CAPTURED AND BECAME A PRISONER OF WAR FOR OVER A YEAR. HE AND I SAT TALKING ALL NIGHT. HE RELATED SOME OF HIS HAUNTING EXPERIENCES AS A POW. I DIDN'T THINK IT APPROPRIATE TO TELL HIM ABOUT MY RECENT, NOT EASILY FORGOTTEN, BUS RIDE OR OF MY WAR TIME STAYS AT THE FAIRMONT HOTEL WITH RICKI.

THE NEXT DAY I ARRIVED IN NEW YORK, THE MOST CHALLENGING, PROGRESSIVE AND EXCITING CITY IN THE WORLD. THE FIRST THING WAS FIND MY WAY TO THE LINCOLN HOTEL AT SEVENTY-SECOND STREET AND BROADWAY TO SEE IF IT'S POLICY OF RENTING ROOMS BY THE WEEK AT A DOLLAR FIFTY A NIGHT WAS TRUE. I DON'T REMEMBER HOW I I FOUND MY WAY TO THE HOTEL, ALL I KNOW, FOR SURE, IS THAT THE LINCOLN HOTEL WAS MY BASE OF OPERATIONS FOR LONG, SOLITARY WEEKS.

MY TIME ALONE IN NEW YORK IS MOSTLY A BLUR. I REMEMBER GENERALLY WHAT I DID AND DIDN'T DO, BUT MOST DETAILS ARE HAZY. I REMEMBER PUSHING MY WAY INTO AUDITIONS, READING FROM A SCRIPT AND LISTENING TO REJECTIONS. I CAN'T BRING TO MIND WHERE I ATE, PRINCIPLY BECAUSE IT IS NOT COMFORTING TO ENVISION THE AUTOMAT AND RECOLLECT ONLY THAT THE FOOD OUT OF THE LOCKED, GLASS FRONTED BOXES WAS CHEAP, PUT TOGETHER TO BE ATTRACTIVE AND APPEALING, AND TOO OFTEN SO VERY DISAPPOINTING. I WALKED EVERYWHERE, TAKING IN THE SIGHTS AND SOUNDS OF THE CITY. I DO, THOUGH, DISTINCTLY RECALL MY SLEEPLESS NIGHTS IN THE LINCOLN HOTEL. THOSE MEMORIES ARE FIXED IN MY MIND BECAUSE THE SOLITUDE, THE FRUSTRATIONS, THE WORRIES, AND THE POSSIBLITY OF FAILURE WERE SO PRESSING. EVERY THIRD NIGHT A CALL TO RICKI HELPED MOMENTARILY. FOR THREE MINUTES, WE WOULD TRY TO CHEER EACH OTHER UP. KNOWING THAT WE WERE EXCHANGING HAPLESS BROMIDES MADE THOSE PHONE CALLS DIFFICULT. WE HAD NOTHING TO SAY THAT WAS INDEPENDENT OF THE CIRCUMSTANCES EXCEPT FOR BITS OF GOOD NEWS ABOUT STEPHEN AND HIS WALKING, RUNNING AND TALKING ABILITIES. THOSE PHONE CALLS MADE EVERY THIRD NIGHT'S PASSING HARD TO MANAGE AND THE NEXT MORNING I'D BE DOG TIRED.

I WAS GETTING CLOSE TO GIVING UP AND I REMEMBER HOW PAINFUL THE THOUGHT OF SURRENDER WAS. I DO RECOLLECT SETTING OUT ON WHAT COULD HAVE BEEN MY LAST OFF-BROADWAY FORAY WITH MIMICKED DETERMINATION AND LITTLE OPTIMISM.

OUTSIDE ONE OF GREENWICH VILLAGE'S INTIMATE THEATRES I STOOD WITH ANOTHER ACTOR COMPLAINING ABOUT NOT FINDING AN ACTING JOB AND RUNNING OUT OF MONEY. I CAN BRING BACK

AMOST WORD FOR WORD OUR CONVERSTION AND WHAT FOLLOWED, BECAUSE IT CHANGED THE WHOLE OF MY STAY IN NEW YORK AND, IT'S SAFE TO SAY, THE REST OF MY LIFE. . HE LOOKED AT ME AND SAID, "IF I LOOKED LIKE YOU, I'D TRY MODELING. IT'S BIG HERE AND PAYS WELL."

HE LEFT AND HIS COMMENT, "PAYS WELL," REMAINED. SOMETHING THAT PAID WELL WAS WORTH INVESTIGATING, SURELY. I KNEW WHAT I LOOKED LIKE, WAS AWARE OF WHAT GENES HAD PROVIDED. WITH CIRCUMSTANCES AS GRIM THEY WERE, I ALSO KNEW THAT I SHOULDN'T FAIL TO TAKE ADVANTAGE OF AN UNACCOUNTABLE GIFT, IF THE GIFT WOULD ALLOW ME TO STAY IN NEW YORK CITY.

A READABLE PHONE BOOK DISCLOSED A SHORT LIST OF MODELING AGENCIES. ONE, "SOCIETY OF MODELS," WAS ON EAST 44TH STREET. SINCE NOTHING OF INTEREST WAS OCCURRING IN THE VILLAGE, I DECIDED TO FIND THE AGENCY ON THE WAY BACK TO THE HOTEL.

THE SOM OFFICE WAS PARTITIONED. THERE WAS A SMALL WAITING AREA, THERE WERE LADIES AT A BANK OF PHONES AND A SEPARATE OPEN-DOORED SPACE PRESIDED OVER BY A YOUNG WOMAN TALKING ANIMATEDLY ON ANOTHER PHONE. SHE LOOKED AT ME, WAVED ME IN AND POINTED AT A CHAIR.

WHEN SHE HAD FINISHED HER CALL SHE ASKED, PLEASANTLY, "WHAT CAN I DO FOR YOU?" I TOLD HER WHY I WAS THERE. SHE LISTENED, HELD OUT A BUSINESS CARD AND SAID, RAPID FIRE, "THIS IS WHAT I WANT YOU TO DO. GO TO THE CARD'S ADDRESS, I'LL HAVE THE PHOTOGRAPHER THERE TO SHOOT HEAD SHOTS AND ONE FULL BODY. SHE'LL SEND ME THE PROOFS AND I'LL SELECT WHAT WE NEED AND ORDER A COMPOSITE MADE AND FIFTY PRINTS. I'LL ARRANGE FOR YOU TO PAY LATER. WHEN I HAVE THE PRINTS, I'LL CALL YOU." I GAVE HER THE HOTEL'S NUMBER AND LEFT IN A DAZE.

THAT'S A SUMMATION OF JOAN WEBSTER'S, OWNER OF SOM, NEW YORK PACED INSTRUCTIONS. I FOLLOWED THEM TO THE LETTER. WHAT ELSE DID I HAVE TO DO?

FOUR OR FIVE DAYS AFTER MY PHOTO SHOOT, JOAN CALLED LEAVING WORD AT THE HOTEL DESK TO COME TO HER OFFICE AT NINE O'CLOCK THE NEXT DAY. I ARRIVED AT THE APPOINTED TIME AND SHE BEGAN WITH SOMETHING THAT WAS A GREETING WHICH WAS FOLLOWED BY MORE INSTRUCTIONS: "GET A FOLDER TO CARRY YOUR PRINTS IN, GO TO THE ADDRESSES LISTED HERE, SHE HANDED ME A PRINTED SHEET, FIND THE PHOTOGRAPHERS NAMED, WALK IN, GIVE YOUR NAME AND HAND OVER YOUR COMPOSITE WITH THE AGENCY'S INFORMATION ON THE BACK. BY THE WAY," SHE ADDED, "HINSEY IS HARD TO REMEMBER. JOHN IS FINE. PICK A LAST NAME THAT'S SIMPLE, STRONG AND EASY TO REMEMBER. WHEN YOU DECIDE, WRITE JOHN WHATEVER ON THE BACK OF THE COMPOSITE ALONG SIDE OUR INFORMATION AND CALL ME SO I CAN TELL THE BOOKING GIRLS WHO YOU ARE."

THAT NIGHT I GAVE A LOT OF THOUGHT TO PICKING A NEW LAST NAME. I WAS PROUD OF MY MIDNIGHT CHOICE: "FLOOD." I COULD HEAR SOMEONE SAY I'M JOHN FLOOD, LIKE IN FLOODLIGHT, A FLOODLIGHT, I THOUGHT, BEING A STOCK PIECE OF EQUIPMENT FOR PHOTOGRAHERS. WHEN I TOLD JOAN THE NEXT DAY ABOUT FLOOD AND FLOODLIGHT SHE LAUGHED AND SAID, "TALK ABOUT EASY."

CHAPTER

9

AT THE END OF MY FIRST WEEK, AS A MALE MODEL I HAD EARNED ALMOST TWO HUNDRED DOLLARS, A FORTUNE IN THE LATE 1940'S. I WAS ECSTATIC OVER THE WINDFALL, BUT WAS NOT FEELING OVERLY SELF-RESPECTING FOR HAVING EARNED THAT KIND OF MONEY BY SIMPLY POSING. I THOUGHT I SHOULD APPEAR PROFESSIONALLY AT EASE WHEN SEEING JOAN SO I WALKED IN WITH A SENSIBLE QUESTION. I ASKED, "DID I DO WELL BECAUSE I WAS THE NEW KID ON THE BLOCK OR CAN I EXPECT MORE GOOD WEEKS?"

SHE REPLIED THAT I WAS A GOOD TYPE, PHOTOGRAHED WELL AND WAS COOPERATIVE. "YOU'LL DO WELL EVERY WEEK," SHE ASSURED ME.

MY FIRST THOUGHT WAS TO CALL RICKI. MY SECOND WAS, I CAN NOW BE IN NEW YORK AND FIND WORK AS AN ACTOR.

THERE WAS A BOOKING LATER AND THEN THE POSSIBILITY OF RICKI COMING TO NEW YORK HAD TO BE DELT WITH. THERE WAS THE QUESTION OF FINDING A MORE PREFERABLE PLACE TO STAY. PICTURING HER WALKING ACROSS THE SO-CALLED LOBBY AT THE $1.50- A- NIGHT LINCOLN HOTEL WAS APPALLING. WHAT ABOUT STEPHEN? WE WOULD NEED TIME TO MAKE PROPER ARRANGEMENTS FOR HIM. I CALLED HER WITHOUT SUFFICIENT ANSWERS. IT WAS A PRICEY CALL. NO THREE MINUTE CONVERSATION THAT NIGHT.

SHE WAS PLEASED WITH THE NEWS OF MY NEW AND HEFTY INCOME, AND MADE A POINT OF SOMETHING THAT HADN'T OCCURRED TO ME. "YOU MADE MORE THAN YOU WOULD HAVE MADE UNDER CONTRACT TO UNIVERSAL." THAT'S TRUE, I CLEARLY REMENBER THINKING, BUT IT WAS ALSO TRUE THAT I'D BE AN ACTOR, NOT A MODEL.

SHE TOLD ME THAT STEPHEN WAS NOT A PROBLEM, THAT HER MOTHER ADORED HIM AND THAT SHE WOULD BE PLEASED TO HAVE HIM ALL TO HERSELF. WE TALKED ON AND ON, GETTING A FIRM GRIP ON WHAT WAS REQUIRDED OF US BECAUSE OF AN INCIDENT IN GREENWICH VILLAGE. RICKI DECIDED TO FLY TO NEW YORK BECAUSE SHE HAD ENOUGH MONEY IN HER SAVINGS ACCOUNT. SHE SAID SHE'D CALL SOM AND THE HOTEL TO LEAVE WORD OF HER FLIGHT AND TIME OF ARRIVAL, TWO VERY HAPPY PEOPLE SAID A HEARTFELT GOODNIGHT.

TWO DAYS LATER I MOVED INTO ONE ROOM ON THE TOP FLOOR OF A GREENWICH VILLAGE TOWN HOUSE ON 12TH STREET, JUST OFF OF 5TH AVENUE. IT BECAME OUR BASE OF OPERATIONS FOR SEVERAL MONTHS. RICKI ARRIVED AND WE SETTLED IN. I WAS HAPPY TO BE, ONCE AGAIN, TOGETHER.

BETWEEN BOOKINGS, I WAS HER PRIVATE TOUR GUIDE. AS I ACQUAINTED HER WITH NEW YORK, I, NOT FOR THE FIRST TIME, WAS AWARE OF ITS SEDUCTIVE POWERS. AS WE RODE THE DOUBLE DECKER BUSES ALONG FIFTH AVENUE I SAW THE RUSHING, HONKING CABS AND THE CROWDED SIDEWALKS EXCITING RATHER THAN ANNOYING. I SAW THE BUILDINGS NOT JUST TALL BUT MAGNIFICENT. WE WENT INTO PLACES I HADN'T BEEN IN, LIKE THE PLAZA HOTEL'S LOBBY AND TIFFANY'S THAT SHINY, SPARKLING JEWELLERY AND I WAS OVERWHELMED. WE HAD A DRINK AT THE BAR OF THE ALGONQUIN HOTEL AND WE TALKED ABOUT IT'S FAMOUS ROUND TABLE GATHERINGS. WE SAW OUR FIRST BROADWAY SHOW. WE EXPLORED THE LENGTH OF CENTRAL PARK, A PLACE OF BEAUTY AND PEACE WHILE SURROUNDED BY COSTLY REAL ESTATE. I TOOK HER INTO THE MUSEUM OF MODERN ART AND SHE LOOKED AT PAINTINGS SHE DIDN'T UNDERSTAND BUT THOUGHT THEY WERE COLORFUL. WE TRAVELED UPTOWN AND DOWNTOWN VIA THE RATTLING SUBWAY. AT NIGHT WE WALKED 8TH STREET IN THE VILLAGE GOING INTO SHOPS AND OFTEN EATING IN A STOREFRONT RESTAURANT, CALLED SEA FAIRE. THEY PUT OUT FRESH FISH, BUT WITHHELD PROMPT SERVICE. I HAD BECOME ACQUAINTED WITH NEW YORK CITY'S EMINENCE AND PRESTIGE AND I'VE NEVER GOTTEN OVER IT.

ON A MONDAY MORNING I TOOK RICKI IN TO MEET JOAN WEBSTER. JOAN SAID SOMETHING THAT RESEMBELED A GREETING, STARED, AND PICKED UP HER HANDY PHONE. SHE TALKED BRIEFLY AND WHILE STILL HOLDING THE PHONE, SAID TO ME, "TAKE RICKI OVER TO PLUCER'S STUDIO AT 480 LEX, HE'S WAITING."

WHEN WE GOT TO THE STREET RICKI ASKED, "WHAT WAS THAT ALL ABOUT?"

I SMILED AND TOLD HER THAT SHE JUST SAW JOAN AT HER NEW YORK BEST, THAT PLUCER WAS A WELL KNOWN COMMERCIAL PHOTOGRAPHER, AND THAT WE SHOULD GO TO HIS STUDIO AND FIND OUT.

AT THE STUDIO, PLUCER CAME OUT AND INTRODUCED HIMSELF TO RICKI AND LED US INTO HIS SHOOTING SPACE. AFTER STUDYING RICKI, HE HELPED HER STAND ON A COUCH AND HANDED HER A CLOSED UMBRELLA AND SAID DO SOMETHING WITH THAT. SHE SMILED AND COMPLETELY AT EASE HELD THE UMBRELLA AT EACH END ACROSS HER THIGHS. HE ASKED HER TO LOOK DIRECTLY INTO THE CAMERA. SHE SHIFTED SLIGHTLY AND, WITH A LOOK I'D NEVER SEEN BEFORE, EYED THE CAMERA. SHE ACTUALLY PREFORMED BUT I COULDN'T READ ANYTHING INTO THE PERFORMANCE, OR TAKE ANYTHING FROM IT. SHE WAS A NATURAL.

LATE THE NEXT DAY JOAN CALLED RICKI AT THE TOWN HOUSE. I WAS OUT "WORKING," AND SAID SHE'D LIKE THE TWO US TO COME IN AT NINE IN THE MORNING. WHEN WE GOT THERE, JOAN WAVED US INTO HER OFFICE POINTED TO A BLOWUP OF RICKI ON PLUCER'S COUCH. I LOOKED DOWN AT THE MOST STRIKING PHOTOGRAPH I'D EVER SEEN. IT WAS INCREDIBLE. RICKI LOOKED STUNNINGLY ALOOF. I STOOD GAPING AT SOMETHING SO REMARKABLE THAT I HAD NOTHING TO SAY. RICKI WAS THE FIRST TO SPEAK, "I'D LIKE TO HAVE THAT, IT'S A GREAT SHOT," WAS ALL SHE SAID.

JOAN WENT BEHIND HER DESK AND SAID, "MAYBE LATER, I'VE PLANS FOR THAT SUCKER." SHE PROCEEDED TO TELL US, IN BRIEF, WHAT SHE WAS GOING TO DO: "I'LL HAVE 8 BY 10 PRINTS MADE AND MAIL THEM TO PEOPLE LIKE PENN, AVEDON AND DHAL-WOLFE. THEN I'LL SIT BACK AND WAIT TO SEE

WHAT HAPPENS." SHE REMINDED ME THAT I HAD AFTERNOON BOOKINGS AND SAID, "CHECK WITH THE GIRLS." SHE SAT DOWN AND PROMPTLY REACHED FOR HER PHONE.

I PICKED UP MY BOOKINGS AND WE LEFT TO HAVE BREAKFAST AT THE LUNCHEONETTE ACROSS 44TH STREET. RICKI HAD LITTLE TO SAY; SHE TOOK IT ALL IN STRIDE. I HAD A PREMONITION, BUT SAID ONLY, JOAN KNOWS WHAT SHE'S DOING LET'S LEAVE THINGS WITH HER.

JOAN, I'M SURE, WAS NOT SURPRISED BY THE NUMBER OF PHONE CALLS THAT CAME IN OVER THE FOLLOWING WEEKS ASKING TO BOOK RICKI VANDUSEN. IT WAS IMMEDIATELY CLEAR THAT JOAN, PLUCER AND HIS PHOTOGRAPH BROUGHT FORTH ELECTRIFYING AND HIGHLY REWARDING RESULTS.

RICKI HAD AN INNATE ABILITY TO MOVE GRACEFULLY BEFORE A CAMERA, EVEN THOUGH SHE WAS NOT THE LEAST BIT SYLPH LIKE. SHE HAD AN INBORN ABILITY TO DELIVER A MANNER THAT WAS DEVOID OF FEELINGS, AND YET GOT YOUR ATTENTION AND HELD IT. SHE HAD, OF COURSE, HER CLASSIC BEAUTY. ALL OF THAT BLENDED TOGETHER MADE HER AN ASTONISHING SUCCESS AS ONE OF THE FIRST SUPERMODELS. SHE WAS A NATURAL.

CHAPTER

10

RICKI WAS ON THE RUN ALL DAY, EVERY DAY. I WAS THE ONE NOW WITH SOME FREE TIME AND I MADE GOOD USE OF IT BY TRYING TO FIND AN APARTMENT SO STEPHEN COULD COME TO NEW YORK. I COULDN'T HELP BECOMING MORE AND MORE CONCERNED ABOUT LEAVING HIM IN CALIFORNIA, EVEN THOUGH I KNEW HE WAS WELL CARED FOR.

DUE TO WARTIME SHORTAGES, RENTS WERE FROZEN AT 1943 LEVELS THROUGHT OUT THE CITY. RENT CONTROL MADE FINDING A TWO OR THREE BEDROOM APARTMENT VIRTUALLY IMPOSSIBLE. PEOPLE WERE NOT ABOUT TO LEAVE HOUSING THAT WAS UNBELIEVABLY CHEAP.

I LOVED THE VILLAGE AND ITS CONFUSING ANGLED STREETS. I RAN AN AD IN THE LOCAL PAPER, THE VILLAGE VOICE, OFFERING A THOUSAND DOLLARS FOR A VALID LEAD TO AN APARTMENT THERE. I RECEIVED NOT ONE RESPONSE.

IT BECAME NECESSARY TO RESEARCH OUTSIDE THE CITY. I HEARD GOOD THINGS ABOUT LONG ISLAND, ESPECIALLY THE NORTH SHORE. SEVERAL PEOPLE TOLD ME THAT MANHASSET WAS VERY NICE AND A MAJOR STOP ON THE LONG ISLAND RAILROAD. IT SOUNDED WORTH A VISIT.

ONE SUNDAY MORNING RICKI AND I WENT TO PENN STATION FOR A RAILROAD JOURNEY OUT TO MANHASSET. I BROUGHT THE NEWYORK TIMES TO READ AND HAD ONLY FINISHED THE THICK FRONT SECTION WHEN WE ARRIVED. THE BULKY TIMES WAS LEFT ON THE SEAT, IT WAS TOO HEAVY TO CARRY AROUND.

NEAR THE STATION THERE WAS A BOHACK'S GROCERY STORE, A DRUG STORE AND A VARIETY OF SMALL SHOPS. ADEQUATE SHOPPING WAS A GOOD SIGN. WE WALKED THE RESIDENTIAL STREETS AND LIKED THE WELL MANTAINED HOUSES. WE SPOTTED A REAL ESTATE OFFICE, WALKED IN TO BE GREETED BY AN OLDER WOMAN. WE TOLD HER WE WOULD LIKE TO LOOK AT THREE BEDROOM RENTALS.

"I DON'T KNOW OF EVEN ONE," SHE SAID. OUR ACUTE DISAPPOINT PROMPTED HER TO ASK IF WE'D CONSIDERED BUYING INSTEAD OF RENTING? SHE SPELLED OUT ALL OF THE ADVANTAGES OF BUYING KINDLY, NOT AS PART OF A SALES PITCH. THEN SHE ASKED BLUNTLY, "WHAT'S YOUR FINANCIAL SITUATION?"

WE TOLD HER OUR OCCUPATIONS, OUR SITUATION AND GAVE HER A BROAD HINT AS TO OUR INCOME. SHE ASKED IF I WAS A VET. I NODDED. SHE SAID, "WITH A GI LOAN YOU COULD EASILY BUY. WHY DON'T WE DO THIS, "I KNOW WHAT YOU NEED, A BED ROOM FOR YOUR SON, ONE FOR A HOUSE KEEPER AND A THIRD FOR THE TWO OF YOU." WE AGREED.

SHE SUGGESTED THAT WE RETURN THE NEXT WEEKEND AND SHE WOULD HAVE A SELECTION OF HOMES FOR US TO LOOK AT. SHE ADDED THAT SHE COULD MAKE RESERVATIONS FOR A SATURDAY NIGHT STAY OVER IF WE'D LIKE TO DO THAT. WE GAVE HER SOM'S PHONE NUMBER AND TOLD HER WE'D CALL FROM PENN STATION WHEN WE KNEW OUR ARRIVAL TIME.

I LEFT MANHASSET THINKING WE HAD TAKEN SOME PROGRESSIVE, BUT ALSO SCARY STEPS, TOWARD SOLVING OUR BIGGEST PROBLEM, GETTING STEPHEN TO NEW YORK.

THE FOLLOWING SATURDAY WE TOURED MANHASSET.

ON SUNDAY AFTERNOON WE WERE SHOWN A HOUSE, NOT IN MANHASSET BUT NEARBY, THAT BOTH OF US LIKED. LET'S MAKE AN OFFER RICKI WHISPERED WHEN WE WERE ALONE IN ONE OF THE BEDROOMS. WE TOLD THE AGENT THAT WE THOUGHT THE HOUSE WOULD WORK FOR US AND WE'D LIKE TO GO BACK TO THE OFFICE TO TALK. AT THE OFFICE THERE WAS A SEAMLESS SEGUE FROM "TO TALK," TO OUR MAKING AN OFFER TO BUY THE HOUSE.

BACK AT THE TOWN HOUSE, RICKI CALLED HER MOTHER AND TOLD HER WE WERE BUYING A HOUSE OUT ON LONG ISLAND AS IF IT WAS A COMMON OCCURRENCE. RICKI HAD A SPECIAL ABILITY TO ACCEPT NEW LIFE-CHANGING DIRECTIONS WITHOUT A QUAM, AS IF WHATEVER DEVELOPED WOULD SOMEHOW BE IN HER FAVOR. I, UNFORTUNATELY, COULD NOT MAKE AN OFFER TO BUY A HOUSE WITHOUT BEING CONCERNED ABOUT SUCH A LONGTERM COMMITMENT AND ALL THE ATTENDANT RESPOSIBILITIES.

IT WAS DIFFICULT TO GET USED TO OUR SWOLLEN INCOME. HOME OWNERSHIP WAS MIND-BOGGLING. AS WAS HAVING A DRINK AT THE STORK CLUB, SYMBOL OF CAFÉ SOCIETY, OR EATING AT SARDI'S, THE FAMOUS THEATRICAL HANGOUT. THIS NEW LIFE WAS OVERWHELMING, YET I WANTED IT TO CONTINUE JUST SO I COULD LIVE AND WORK IN A CITY THAT I HAD FALLEN IN LOVE WITH, WARTS AND ALL. I LOVED ITS BUSTLE, ITS CYNICISM AND ITS BAD MANNERS. I WAS WHERE I WANTED TO BE.

OUR OFFER WAS ACCEPTED. WE FURNISHED IT WITH HELP AND HIRED A MARVELOUS LIVE IN, IDA RANKIN. RICKI'S MOTHER BROUGHT STEPHEN TO US. A JEEP STATION WAGON GOT US TO THE TRAIN STATION. WE COMMUTED TO THE CIY MONDAY THROUGH FRIDAY AND THE MONEY, IN EXCEPTIONAL AMOUNTS, KEPT ROLLING IN. I MODELED FOR THE MONEY, BUT WORKED HARD AT TRYING TO ESTABLISH AN ACTING CAREER. I READ FOR AND GOT A GOOD ROLE IN A TV PROGRAM, HOSTED BY NEIL HAMILTON, THAT SHOWCASED NEW TALENT. THERE WERE ENCOURAGING REACTIONS AND LOTS OF ACTIVITY. NOTHING, HOWEVER, OF CONSEQUENCE DEVELOPED.

SEVERAL MONTHS PAST BY BEFORE I DECIDED IT WAS TIME TO INDULGE IN A SELF-ANALYSIS SESSION. TO BEGIN, I AGREED TO MY HAVING A CERTAIN AMOUNT OF ACTING ABILITY. BUT WAS IT ENOUGH? WAS I GOOD ENOUGH TO SUCCEED? DID I THINK I COULD PROJECT A POSITIVE PRESENCE ON STAGE OR ON THE SILVER SCREEN? WAS A HANDSOME BUT CHARACTERLESS APPEARANCE ENOUGH TO STRIKE IT RICH IN HOLLYWOOD? AND, I THOUGHT, WAS AN ACTING CAREER SOMETHING I WANTED DEPERATATELY? THE ANSWERS WERE ALL NO'S. I WANTED A CAREER IN TELEVISION, AND FINALLY I KNEW WHAT IT WAS. I DECIDED TO SHIFT GOALS FROM ACTING TO TELEVISION PRODUCTION, CONCENTRATING ON DIRECTING.

THROUGH CONNECTIONS, I WAS GIVEN PERMISSION TO SIT IN ON THE REHEARSALS OF GERTRUDE STIEN'S PLAY "YES IS FOR EVERY YOUNG MAN" AT THE CHERRY LANE THEATRE IN THE VILLAGE TO WATCH AND LISTEN TO THE DIRECTOR. THE INDULGENT ANALYSIS BECAME IMPORTANT FOR I WAS BUSY AND DETERMINED TO CHANGE COURSE, HOWEVER, I COULDN'T GET PAST WHATEVER OR WHEREVER THE BARRIERS WERE.

CHAPTER

11

WE INCREASED THE SIZE OF OUR FAMILY BY ONE. WE BECAME PARENTS TO A BEAUTIFUL, BABY GIRL ON AUGUST 30TH, 1950. SHE WAS NAMED DARRAGH CHRISTINE. DARRAGH WAS A IRRESTIBLE NAME I'D HEARD JUST BEFORE SHE WAS BORN.

WE MADE FRIENDS OF PEOPLE OF DIVERSE OCCUPATIONS ON THE ISLAND. I PLAYED WEEKEND BASEBALL ON LONG ISLAND ESTATES BIG ENOUGH TO HAVE A FIELD AND BENCHES FOR VISITORS. I SWAM AND SCUBA DIVED IN THE VERY COLD WATERS OF LONG ISLAND SOUND AND CONSIDERED BUYING A BOAT. STEPHEN HAD LITTLE FRIENDS TO PLAY WITH.

THE DAYS AND WEEKS PASSED BY ROUTINELY, BUT THEN THERE WAS AN UNEXPECTED, DISTURBING LATE NIGHT PHONE CALL FROM TONY WEBSTER, JOAN'S HUSBAND. TONY WAS CRYING AND HARD TO UNDERSTAND, BUT I FINALLY MADE OUT WHAT HE WAS TRYING TO SAY: JOAN HAD LOST THEIR BABY. WE KNEW HOW MUCH THEY'D WANTED A CHILD AND HOW HAPPY THEY WERE WHEN THEY LEARNED JOAN WAS PREGNANT. I ASKED IF HE WAS HOME AND HE SAID NO HE WAS AT THE HOSPITAL AND JOAN WAS DEVASTATED BY THE LOSS. HE STOPPED CRYING AND SAID CLEARLY, THIS IS A LOW, LOW BLOW AND HUNG UP. THERE WAS NOTHING WE COULD DO. WE DIDN'T KNOW WHICH HOSPITAL SHE WAS IN. A FEW DAYS LATER WE LEARNED JUST HOW LOW THE BLOW HAD BEEN. JOAN HAD MISCARRIED TWICE. WE HADN'T KNOWN THAT, SO A WEEK AT HOME TO RECOVER WAS APPROPRIATE, BUT THE WEEK STRETCHED INTO A MONTH. JOAN RETURNED TO SOM, BUT NEVER FULLY REGAINED HER OLD DRIVE OR WILLINGNESS TO WORK HARD AND FAST. ONE DAY, WITHOUT WARNING, SHE CLOSED THE AGENCY. IT WAS A SAD HAPPENING FOR A LOT OF PEOPLE. JOAN AND TONY COULD NOT BE REACHED. WE CALLED GETTING NO ANSWER. WE WENT TO THEIR APARTMENT, IT WAS EMPTY. WE HAD TO ADJUST TO THE SITUATION.

RICKI KNEW EILEEN FORD, OF THE FORD MODELING AGENCY, BY REPUTATION, NEVER HAVING MET HER. EILEEN KNEW RICKI BY FACE AND REPUTATION AND WHEN THEY MET EILEEN WAS HAPPY, INDEED, TO REPRESENT HER. OUR LIVES RETURNED TO OUR CUSTOMARY DAYS AND WEEKS EXCEPT FOR ONE CHANGE: I QUIT POSING, GRATEFULLY. I CONCENTRATED ON OVERCOMING THE BARRIERS TO A JOB OF SOME KIND IN TELEVISION PRODUCTION OR PROGRAMING.

CHAPTER

12

I SOON MADE IT OVER THOSE OBSTACLES IN THE MOST UNCONVENTIONL, MOST BIZARRE WAY THAT CAN BE IMAGINED. IF WHAT HAPPENED WAS A PLOT POINT IN A PLAY IT WOULD HAVE BEEN WRITEN OUT AS, TOO, UNBELIEVABLE.

EILEEN HAD ARRANGED A THREE DAY SHOOT FOR RICKI AT MARSHLL FIELD'S, CHICAGO'S WELL KNOWN DEPARTMENT STORE. WE WERE A LITTLE LATE GETTING TO THE LAGUARDIA AIRPORT AND WERE RUSHING TO FIND RICKI'S FLIGHT. WE TURNED AT A CORNER AND I RAN INTO A MAN HARD ENOUGH TO KNOCK HIM AND HIS BRIEFCASE TO THE FLOOR. I REACHED DOWN TO SEE IF HE WAS ALL RIGHT AND LOOKED INTO THE FACE OF GEORGE HEINEMANN. I ASKED IF HE WAS HURT. HE SAID, "NO, GET ME THE HELL UP." I GOT HIM TO HIS FEET AND LOCATED HIS BRIEFCASE. I KNEW GEORGE AS A COORDINATOR FOR A MAJOR PHOTOGRAPHER. HE WAS EARLY FOR HIS FLIGHT SO WE AGREED TO MEET FOR COFFEE AFTER RICKI WAS SETTLED ON HER PLANE. WE MET AT THE SMALL LUNCH AREA. WE CHATTED. HE TOLD ME THAT HE WAS NOW PROGRAM MANAGER OF NBC'S TELEVISION STATION IN CHICAGO. I TOLD HIM ALL THAT I HAD DONE TO SECURE A FUTURE IN TELEVISION. HE ASKED IF I'D COME TO CHICAGO.

I ANSWERED, "TO AN OUTPOST IN GREENLAND IF THAT WAS NECESSARY TO GET A JOB."

HE LOOKED AT HIS WATCH AND ASKED, "ARE YOU STILL LIVING OUT ON LONG ISLAND?"

I TOLD HIM, "YES."HE ASKED FOR OUR TELEPHONE NUMBER. I GAVE IT TO HIM.

HE SAID, "I'LL CALL."

I DROVE HOME THINKING THE ENCOUNTER WEIRD, NEVER EXPECTING TO HEAR FROM HIM. I'D HEARD TOO MANY TIMES, "I'LL CALLYOU." THIS TIME IT WAS WITHOUT ITS PREFACE, "DON'T CALL ME." THE RESULT, HOWEVER, WOULD BE THE SAME.

WHEN RICKI GOT HOME, I TOLD HER ABOUT MY CONVERSATION WITH GEORGE.

SHE SAID, "I HAD A CUP OF COFFEE WITH GEORGE AND TALKED TO HIM, TOO."

I ASKED, "IF HE CALLS, AND THERE'S A CHANCE TO GO TO WORK THERE, WOULD YOU BE WILLING TO LEAVE NEW YORK AND YOUR CAREER BEHIND? CHICAGO IS NOT 'THE BIG APPLE.' "

RICKI REPLIED, "I KNOW. I JUST SPENT TIME THERE AND I DIDN'T FIND IT AS BAD AS YOU'VE DESCRIBED IT. BESIDES I'M TIRED, AND GIVING UP MY SO CALLED CAREER IS MEANINGLESS TO ME. I'D LIKE SOME FREE TIME TO BE A FULL TIME MOTHER TO MY KIDS."

"YOU DON'T LIKE THE WINTERS HERE. IN CHICAGO THERE CAN BE LONG OVERCAST DAYS WITH PILES OF DIRTY SNOW, THICK ICE THAT COVERS EVERYTHING, WINDS THAT'LL KNOCK YOU DOWN AND TEMPERTURES BELOW ZERO."

"LOOK" SHE SAID, "YOU KNOW THE CITY. YOU'LL FIND US A NICE APARTMENT OR WE COULD BUY A HOUSE TO LIVE IN AND ON DAYS OR WEEKS LIKE THAT I WON'T GO OUT. IT COULD BE FUN. IF YOU CAN FIND A PLACE THAT SUITS YOU IN TELEVISION THERE, YOU'RE THE ONE WHO WILL HAVE TO DEAL WITH THE WINTERS, NOT ME."

I WAS BOTH STUNNED AND DELIGHTED BY HER ATTITUDE.

AFTER MY KNOCKDOWN, I DID, FINALLY, HEAR FROM GEORGE. HE CALLED TO TELL ME THAT HE HAD A PROBLEM AND THAT I MIGHT BE THE SOLUTION. HE ASKED IF I'D HEARD OF, OR SEEN, A PROGRAM TITLED, "KUKLA, FRAN AND OLLIE."

I TOLD HIM I KNEW IT WAS ORIGINALLY A PUPPET SHOW FOR CHILDREN, AND THAT IT HAD GAINED A HUGE ADULT AUDIENCE. I ADDED THAT I'D SEEN IT AND THOUGHT IT BRILLANT.

HE SAID, "GOOD." HE WENT ON TO EXPLAIN THAT BURR TILLSTROM, THE MAN BEHIND THE SHOW, INSISTES THAT ANYONE HE WORKS WITH TREAT HIS PUPPETS AS REAL PEOPLE. AND, GEORGE ADDED, "NO ONE I HAVE AVAILABLE HAS SATISFIED THAT DEMAND. I CAN'T TELL YOU WHY, ALL I KNOW IS THAT HE CONDUCTS SOME KIND OF INTERVIEW-TEST. WOULD YOU BE WILLING TO COME TO CHICAGO, MEET WITH BURR AND IF YOU PASS YOU'D BE THE SHOW'S STAGE MANAGER AT THE START OF THE NEW SEASON FOR ONE YEAR."

I SAID, "I'LL LEAVE TONIGHT AND BE IN YOUR OFFICE AT NINE O'CLOCK."

HIS FINAL COMMENT WAS, "TOO EARLY, GET HERE AROUND 2:30."

I CAUGHT A SEVEN O'CLOCK FLIGHT OUT OF LAGUARDIA AND CHECKED INTO THE SHERMAN HOTEL TO GET A GOOD NIGHT'S SLEEP. I CALLED MY FOLKS AFTER MY MORNING SHOWER TO TELL THEM I WAS IN TOWN AND WHY. THEY WISHED ME LUCK AND I WENT OUT TO WALK THE FAMILIAR STREETS. PROMPTLY AT 2:30, I WAS AT THE MERCHANDISE MART AND IN GEORGE'S OFFICE. HE SHOWED ME AROUND THE STATION'S VAST SPACE WHERE BOTH LOCAL AND NETWORK SHOWS ORIGINATED. IT WAS IMPRESSIVE. AT 3:30 HE WALKED WITH ME TO A MODEST STUDIO, TINY IN FACT. INSIDE, I COULD SEE THE VERY SMALL KUKLA, FRAN AND OLLIE STAGE WITH ITS PROSCENIUM ARCH. GEORGE KNOCKED ON A SIDE DOOR AND WE WALKED INTO BURR TILLSTROM'S OFFICE. I WAS INTRODUCED AS JOHN HINSEY - I'D TOLD GEORGE TO DROP THE "FLOOD." HE LEFT.

BURR WAS VERY PLEASANT. WE WENT INTO THE STUDIO AND HE POINTED TO A FOLDING CHAIR. "WHY DON'T YOU SIT THERE," WAS ALL HE SAID. HE WENT BEHIND THE STAGE. SHORTLY, KUKLA APPEARED AND SAID, "HELLO JOHN HINSEY, I'M KUKLA."

I TOLD KUKLA THAT I WAS HONORED TO MEET SUCH A BIG TELEVISION STAR.

THAT IS HOW OUR CONVERSATION STARTED. I TALKED TO BURR'S "PEOPLE" FOR ABOUT FIFTEEN MINUTES. I ADAPTED QUICKLY TO THE SITUATION AND ENJOYED EXCHANGING POINTS OF VIEW WITH BURR'S CHARMING LITTLE FRIENDS.

KUKLA ENDED OUR GET-TOGETHER BY SAYING SOMETHING LIKE I'VE GOT THINGS TO DO NOW, JOHN. IT WAS NICE MEETING YOU.

BURR CAME OUT THROUGH THE CURTAIN STAGE-LEFT AND SAID, SERIOUSLY, "THEY LIKE YOU. YOU CAN START NEXT WEEK IF YOU THINK YOU WOULD BE HAPPY HERE."

I SAID, "THANK YOU, BURR, I'D BE MORE THAN HAPPY. I ENJOYED TALKING WITH KUKLA AND THE GANG." HE SMILED, NODDED AND WENT INTO HIS OFFICE.

I KNOCKED A MAN DOWN IN THE LA GUARDIA AIRPORT AND THAT HEAD-ON EXPANDED INTO A MOST IMPORTANT, MOST CONSEQUENTIAL HAPPENING THAT MADE A DESIRE FOR CHANGE A REALITY. NBC HIRED ME AND I WAS BURR TILLSTROM'S STAGE MANAGER FOR TWENTY-SIX WEEKS. "STAGE MANAGER" SOUNDS IMPRESSIVE, BUT IT WAS A REQUIREMENT OF TELEVISION'S RULES AND MY ONLY RESPOSIBILITY WAS TO STICK MY HAND THROUGH THAT STAGE-LEFT CURTAIN TO CUE BURR THAT THEY WERE ON THE AIR. AND THEN TO CUE HIM THAT THEY WERE OFF THE AIR. I KNEW THE PUPPETS HAD TO BE HANGING ON HANDY HOOKS, BUT NEVER SAW THEM IN THAT LIFELESS STATE. I SAT, ALONG WITH A SMALL AUDIENCE, DURING THE BROADCAST MESMERIZED BY THE MASTERFUL, IMPROVISATIONAL SKILLS OF FRAN ALLISON WHO CHATTED WITH THE "PEOPLE," JACK FASCINATO WHO FOLLOWED BURR AND FRAN'S LEAD WITH BEFITTING PIANO MELODIES AND, OF COURSE, BURR.

THESE THREE NEVER REHEARSED WITH A SCRIPT. THEY CAME IN TO THAT SMALL STAGE AT ABOUT FOUR O'CLOCK AND FRAN AND GANG CHATTED. THEY HAD A GOOD TIME. THAT'S WHEN I HAD A ROLE TO PLAY. I LAUGHED AT THEIR JOKES, REACTED TO THEIR SQUABLES, MADE INNOCUOUS COMMENTS AND HAD A GOOD TIME, TOO. CLOSE TO FIVE O'CLOCK THE THREE OF THEM WOULD GO INTO BURR'S OFFICE, EMERGE JUST BEFORE SIX AND DO A HALF-HOUR SHOW THAT ALWAYS HAD A BEGINNING, MIDDLE AND AN END. HOW THEY ARRIVED AT AN OUTLINE FOR THAT NIGHT'S SHOW WAS A MYSTERY BECAUSE NO ONE, OTHER THAN THOSE THREE, WAS EVER IN THAT OFFICE AT PRESHOW TIME.

I WAS COMMITTED TO THE KUKLA FRAN AND OLLIE PROGRAM FROM THREE TO SIX-THIRTY, MONDAY THROUGH FRIDAY. MORNINGS, EARLY AFTERNOONS, EVENINGS AND WEEKENDS, GEORGE HAD ME DIRECTING LOCAL SHOWS.

RICKI HAD STAYED IN NEW YORK TO OVERSEE THE SELLING OF THE HOUSE. I FOUND A SPACIOUS APARTMENT IN EVANSTON, (I WAS FINALLY TO LIVE CLOSE TO NORTWESTERN UNIVERSITY) THE FOUR of US WERE A FAMILY THREE MONTHS AFTER MY ARRIVAL IN CHICAGO. RICKI SEEMED CONTENT TO BE A HOUSEWIFE.

MY TWENTY-SIX WEEK COMMITMENT TO BURR TILLSTROM ENDED AND I WAS SORRY IT HAD. I WOULD MISS THE INTIMATE GET-TOGETHERS AND THE FASCINATING AD-LIBBED SHOWS. NEVERTHELESS, I HAD BOTH FEET IN THE PREVIOUSLY CLOSED AND LOCKED TELEVEVISION DOOR AND HAD TO MAKE THE BEST OF IT.

CHAPTER

13

I

DIRECTED, AT ONE TIME OR ANOTHER, ALL OF THE LOCAL SHOWS AND THEN ONE FINE DAY I WAS APPOINTED THE DIRECTOR OF A NEW SOAP OPERA CALLED "THE BENNETS," SCHEDULED FOR MONDAY THROUGH FRIDAY ON THE NETWORK. OUR INITIAL AIRING GOT GOOD REVIEWS BUT GOOD RATINGS DIDN'T FOLLOW. THE SHOW HAD A SHORT RUN AND WAS CANCELLED. THE CANCELLATION SERVED AS A WAKEUP-CALL.

WHEN I WAS HIRED, NBC'S OWNED AND OPERATED STATION IN CHICAGO, SUPPLIED THE NETWORK WITH A NUMBER OF HIGHLY RATED SHOWS: GARROWAY AT LARGE, STUD'S PLACE, MARLIN PERKINS' ZOO PARADE, HAWKINS FALLS AND KUKLA FRAN AND OLLIE AMONG OTHERS. THERE WAS THE PROMISE OF A BRIGHT FUTURE. SOME WERE ALREADY OFF THE AIR. THE BENNETS' CANCELLATION BROUGHT THAT NUMBER DOWN ONE MORE. IT GRADUALLY BECAME CLEAR THAT NETWORK ORIGINATIONS WOULD OCCUR ONLY IN NEW YORK AND LOS ANGELES. I TALKED TO RICKI ABOUT CHICAGO BECOMING A DEAD END AND THAT WE SHOULD RETURN TO NEW YORK OR LOS ANGELES. AFTER LIVING IN THE WINDY CITY FOR ALMOST THREE YEARS, RICKI LIKED CHICAGO ONLY SLIGHTLY MORE THAN MY MOTHER, SO THE DECISION TO LEAVE WAS NOT AN ISSUE, BUT WHICH WAY TO GO, EAST OR WEST WAS. RICKI SAID, "LET'S GO HOME," MEANING SOUTHERN CALIFORNA. THOUGH I FAVORED NEW YORK, THE THOUGHT OF LOTS OF BLUE SKY AND WARM SUNSHINE MADE IT EASY TO AGREE.

I WENT TO GEORGE'S OFFICE TO TELL HIM OF OUR DECISION TO LEAVE. HIS REACTION SURPRISED ME. "I KNOW WHY YOU'RE LEAVING AND IT'S GOOD THAT YOU'RE TOO SMART TO GET STUCK HERE. I'M DOING EVERY THING I CAN TO GET TRANSFERRED TO NEW YORK. THAT'S WHERE THE ACTION WILL BE. WHERE ARE YOU GOING?"

I TOLD HIM THAT I'D LOVE TO GO BACK TO NEW YORK. BUT RICKI WANTED TO GO HOME, SO IT'S LOS ANGELES FOR US.

"L.A. IS JUST AS GOOD," HE SAID. THEN ADDED, "YOU HAVE TO GO UP AND SEE JULES THOUGH, HE'LL HATE IT THAT YOU'RE LEAVING." WE SHOOK HANDS AND WISHED EACH OTHER LUCK.

JULES, THE STATION MANAGER, WAS FAR FROM HAPPY WHEN I TOLD HIM I WAS THERE TO SAY GOODBYE. HE SAID, "I THINK YOU'RE MAKING A MISTAKE AND YOU'LL WANT TO COME BACK. I'LL HAVE A LEAVE OF ABSENCE PREPARED AND WE'LL SIGN IT BEFORE YOU LEAVE."

I THANKED HIM AND WENT DOWNSTAIRS TO GATHER MY BELONGINGS AND SAY GOODBYE TO THE PEOPLE WHO WERE IN THAT DAY.

WE SPENT THE NEXT WEEK GETTING READY TO MOVE BACK TO THE EVEN TEMPERATURES OF THE WEST COAST. THE MOVE WAS A HARROWING STRUGGLE. WE LEFT CHICAGO EXHAUSTED.

RICKI'S SISTER, MARY, MET THE FOUR OF US AT LAX AND WE STAYED WITH HER UNTIL WE HAD AN AGENDA WITH PRIORITIES. WE HAD A RESERVE OF CASH, SO INSTEAD OF RENTING WE OPTIMISTICALLY BOUGHT A RANCH STYLE, THREE BEDROOM HOUSE IN A NEW COMMUNITY NEAR MARY. A QUICK ESCROW HAD US MOVING IN WITH OUR FURNITURE FROM CHICAGO. I PURCHASED WHAT WAS EMBLEMATIC OF SOUTHERN CALIFORNIA, A SNAZZY WHITE WITH RED INTERIOR CONVERTABLE AND SET OUT WITH THE TOP DOWN TO FIND A JOB. I WENT TO CBS AND ABC, WITH RESUME', TO LEARN THEY WEREN'T HIRING DIRECTORS, THEY WERE FULLY STAFFED. I FOUND MY LEAVE OF ABSENCE PAPERS, DROVE TO NBC'S NETWORK OFFICES AT SUNSET AND VINE, AND TALKED TO THE PERSONNEL OFFICER, WHO SEEMED INTERESTED. HE EXTENDED THE USUAL, LET ME MAKE A FEW PNONE CALLS, YOU'LL HEAR FOM ME. I KNEW OF AT LEAST ONE PHONE CALL, TO CHICAGO.

THE NEXT DAY HE CALLED TO TELL ME TO COME IN AT TWO PM AND GO TO BOB CORWIN'S OFFICE. I MET MR. CORWIN ONLY TO HAVE HIM TELL ME THAT WITH MY SOLID BACKGROUND THEY'D LIKE TO HAVE ME ON STAFF, BUT NOT AS A DIRECTOR, AS A STAGE MANAGER. HE EXPLAINED THEY HAD A FIRM POLICY THAT FUTURE DIRECTORS START AT THE STAGE MANAGER LEVEL AND WORK THEIR WAY UP.

BOB DIDN'T APPEAR TO BE VERY BUSY SO WE TALKED FOR A WHILE. MY QUESTIONS AND HIS ANSWERS DID NOTHING TO GET AROUND THE POLICY. IT WAS, INDEED, IRONCLAD. THERE WAS NO WAY OF KNOWING HOW LONG I'D BE A STAGE MANAGER, BUT IT WAS A JOB THAT I COULD BE FREE OF AT ANY TIME. THERE WAS NO COMITTMENT, LIKE WITH BURR TILLSTROM. I DECIDED THEN AND THERE, SECOND THOUGHTS WERE FOR LATER, TO TAKE THE JOB.

A PHONE CALL AND A MEETING COMBINED TO BECOME A LIFE-CHANGING EVENT AND THE START OF A WEST COAST CAREER IN TELEVISION.

CHAPTER

14

MY FIRST ASSIGNMENT WAS THE FIFTEEN MINUTE DINAH SHORE SHOW. IT AIRED THREE DAYS A WEEK IN STUDIO "D" AT SUNSET AND VINE. THERE WAS A FULL ORCHESTRA, AN AUDIENCE SECTION AND PERFORMING GUESTS. THE SHOW WAS VERY POPULAR AND SPONSORED BY CHEVROLET. I DIDN'T SIT TO WATCH AND LISTEN LIKE IN CHICAGO. I GUIDED DINAH TO HER MARKS, CUED HER AND THE ORCHESTRA, GOT THE GUEST IN PLACE AND AFTER EACH NUMBER WAVED THE AUDIENCE INTO A FRENZY OF APPLAUSE.

I MOVED ON TO STAGE MANAGE THE COLGATE COMEDY HOUR, THIS IS YOUR LIFE AND HALLMARK HALL OF FAME, ALL WITH A GREAT DEAL MORE RESPONSIBILITY. I WAS EXPECTING A NOTICE OF ADVANCEMENT WHEN NBC ANNOUNCED A NEW POLICY. THEY WOULD NO LONGER HAVE STAFF DIRECTORS. THEY WOULD HIRE AS NEEDED. WELL, TO ME, THAT WAS NOT A POLICY, IT WAS A FAIT ACCOMPLI. THE IDEA OF QUITING AND ENTERING A POOL OF DIRECTORS WITH MY ONE NETWORK CREDIT AND THAT OF A SHOW THAT FAILED WAS NOT A WISE MOVE. THE IDEA OF BEING A STAGE MANAGER FOR THE REST OF MY LIFE WASN'T IN THE LEAST ALLURING EITHER. I WAS FACED WITH ANOTHER DEAD END. IT WAS A BLOW THAT FORCED A SHIFT IN PLANS.

THE INTEGRATING OF ALL THE VARIOUS ASPECTS OF A SHOW HAD ALWAYS BEEN FASCINATING. NBC STAFFED PRODUCTION MANGERS; I'D MET MOST OF THEM. DUE TO THE NEW CIRCUMSTANCES, I THOUGHT PRODUCTION MANAGER COULD BE THE SOLUTION.

NBC IN SOUTHERN CALIFORNIA WAS BY NOW A GIANT OPERATION ON THIRTY-FOUR ACRES IN BURBANK, CALIFORNIA. THERE WAS A BIG, TWO STORIED ADMINISTRATION BUILDING, MAMMOTH STAGES, REHEARSAL HALLS, HUGE AREAS TO BUILD SETS AND PAINT DROPS, WARDROBE AREAS TO MAKE AND STORE COSTUMES, PROP STORAGE, WORK SHOPS OF EVERY DISCRIPTION.

NBC WAS OWNED BY THE RADIO CORPORATION OF AMERICA HEADED BY GENERAL DAVID SARNOFF. ONE OF HIS SONS, TOM SARNOFF, WAS A WEST COAST V.P. I KNEW TOM BECAUSE HE USED TO VISIT THE HALLMARK HALL FAME SETS. I'D SHOW HIM AROUND, INTRODUCE HIM TO THE CURRENT STAR AND WE'D HAVE A CUP COFFEE TOGETHER. HE WAS A PLEASANT, LIKEABLE GUY. I CALLED HIS OFFICE AND ASKED FOR AN APPOINTMENT AND WAS GIVEN A TIME.

IN BRIEF, I TOLD TOM MY SITUATION AND ASKED HIM BLUNTLY IF HE'D HELP ME TRANSFER TO PRODUCTION MANAGING. HE DIDN'T HESITATE. LET ME MAKE A CALL, THEN GO DOWN AND A SEE GEORGE HABIB IN ROOM WHAT EVER IT WAS. I MET GEORGE AND REPEATED MY REASONS FOR WANTING TO SWITCH TO PRODUCTION MANAGING. HE SAID, "UNDER THE CIRCUMSTANCES, I THINK YOU"RE MAKING A WISE MOVE." AND WITH THAT I WAS TRANSFERRED TO THE CARE AND HANDLING OF GEORGE HABIB.

THE BURBANK FACILITIES WERE KEPT BUSY BY PROJECTS PRESENTED BY OUSIDE PRODUCERS, DIRECTORS, WRITERS, STARS AND AGENCIES THAT PACKAGED SHOWS AND SOME WERE PRODUCED FROM WITHIN NBC. THE FACILITES WERE MADE AVAILABLE FOR WHAT EVER WAS NEEDED TO GET THE SHOWS ON THE AIR. A PRODUCTION MANAGER WAS ASSIGNED TO ASSURE THAT WHAT WAS NEEDED WAS PROVIDED AND TO ACCOMPLISH THAT WITHIN A BUDGET. THE JOB WAS CHALLENGING AND FULFILLING. THERE WERE INTERESTING AND TALENTED MEN AND WOMEN TO MEET AND OFFER ASSISTANCE. I HELPED ORGANIZE A FIVE-A-WEEK, DAYTIME, ONE HOUR DRAMATIC SERIES CALLED, "MATINEE THEATRE," AND THEN BECAME ONE OF ITS PRODUCERS. AFTER THAT STINT, MY NEXT MOVE WAS TO JOIN MANAGEMENT AND BECOME A FILM PROGRAMMING MANAGER. FILM MANAGERS WORKED WITH PRODUCERS, APPROVED OR DISAPPROVED SUBMITTED SCRIPT OUTLINES, SUGGESTED CHANGES, IF NECESSARY, IN FIRST DRAFT SCRIPTS, FOLLOWED AN EPISODE'S PROGRESS TO FILM AND REVIEWED THE FIRST CUT FILM AND THE FINAL CUT. NBC SAUGHT QUALITY IN EVERY SHOW ON ITS NETWORK. IT WASN'T LONG BEFORE I WAS GIVEN A LARGER OFFICE NAMED DIRECTOR OF FILM MANAGING IN CHARGE OF SIX FILM MANAGERS. THEN, I WAS MADE HEAD OF FILM DEVELOPMENT. WITH EACH NEW POSITION, I DID MY BEST TO MEET THE DEMANDS OF EACH POSITION'S NEW SET OF RESPOSIBILITIES. I WAS A HAPPY, HARD WORKING PROGRAM EXECUTIVE.

ON MARCH 4, 1965, A MEMORABLE DAY, GRANT TINKER, V.P. IN CHARGE OF WEST COAST OPERATIONS, SLATHERED ICING ON MY CAKE BY APPOINTING ME THE HEAD OF NBC PRODUCTIONS WHICH WAS UNEXPECTED, ASTONISHING AND THRILLING. THE NEXT MORNING I PICKED UP MY "DAILY VARIETY," ONE OF TWO DALIES, THAT KEPT EVERYONE AWARE OF WHAT WAS HAPPENING IN HOLLYWOOD'S BUSINESS OF TELEVISION AND MOVIE MAKING, AND ON THE FIRST PAGE THERE WAS AN ARTCLE HEADED BY "NBC-TV UPTEMPS OWN PROD'N HERE; HINSEY HELMS OPERATION." IT WENT ON TO TELL HOW NBC WAS TO ORIGINATE FILM PROGRAMS TO HELP FILL THE NETWORK'S PROGRAMMING SCHEDULE WTH ITS OWN PRODUCT. WHAT IT DIDN'T SAY WAS TO HAVE NBC REAP THE PROFITS FROM SYNDICATION THAT WOULD COME AFTER A SHOW'S SUCCESSFUL RUN ON THE NETWORK.

GRANT AND I SELECTED THREE SCRIPTS SUBMITTED TO NBC PRODUCTIONS THAT WERE WRITTEN BY HARRY JULIAN FINK, BUCK HENRY AND WILLIAM PETER BLATTY TO SERVE AS PILOTS FOR THE NETWORK. GRANT SENT THE MATERIAL OFF TO NEW YORK FOR THEIR APPROVAL TO PROCEED. THEY WERE APPROVED WITH HIGH PRAISE. NO ONE IN NEW YORK THOUGHT THAT NBC PRODUCTIONS COULD FIND EVEN ONE OUTSTANDING SCRIPT IN THE FIRST YEAR SO THREE HAD TO BE CONSIDERED A PORTENT OF UNPRECEDENTED SUCCESS.

DON RICKLES WAS ALREADY SET AS THE LEAD FOR THE BILL BLATTY SCRIPT TITLED, "PLOTKIN PRISON." RICHARD WOOKEY, OUR CASTING DIRECTOR, WORKED DILIGENTLY TO FIND US SUITABLE LEADS IN HOLLYWOOD FOR THE HARRY JULIAN FINK SCRIPT TITLED, "T.H.E. CAT," AND THE BUCK HENRY SCRIPT

TITLED, "CAPTAIN NICE." HE DIDN'T FIND ANY ONE WHO WAS AVAILABLE AND RIGHT. RICHARD AND I CONTINUED THE SEARCH IN LAS VEGAS, CHICAGO AND NEW YORK. IN NEW YORK, ROBERT LOGGIA WAS SIGNED FOR T.H.E. CAT, AND WILLIAM DANIELS FOR CAPTAIN NICE. I CAME BACK TO CALIFORNIA, FOUND OFFICE SPACE AT PARAMOUNT STUDIOS AND BEGAN TO MAKE SURE THAT EACH PROJECT HAD ALL THAT WAS NEEDED TO BEGIN FILMING. IT HAD BEEN DECIDED TO SHOOT PART OF "T.H.E. CAT" IN SAN FRANCISCO. ALL OF THOSE ARRAGEMENTS WERE MADE EFFICIENTLY IN BURBANK.

AFTER PREPRODUCTION MEETINGS I HAD TIME TO DAYDREAM AND LOOK AHEAD. IF EVEN JUST ONE PROJECT WENT ON THE AIR AND HAD A LONG RUN, I, THE HEAD OF NBC PRODUCTIONS, COULD REAP UNBELIEVABLE BENEFITS. NBC PRODUCTIONS COULD EXPAND, I COULD BECOME A VICE PRESIDENT, OR I COULD FORM MY OWN INDEPENDENT PRODUCTION COMPANY. THAT WAS HEADY STUFF, INDEED.

CHAPTER

15

TELEVISION, THOUGH, DID NOT DOMINATE MY LIFE. A GOOD PART OF ME WAS DEVOTED TO HEARTH AND HOME. RICKI WAS CONTENT TO BE A HOUSEWIFE. THERE WERE FAMILY AFFAIRS TO DEAL WITH. STEPHEN PLAYED FOOTBALL AND BASEBALL IN HIGH SCHOOL. I ATTENDED EVERY GAME THAT I COULD. DARRAGH'S SPARE TIME WAS SPENT WITH HER UNCLE RALPH'S HORSES. RALPH HAD A BOAT MOORED IN NEWPORT AND WE WOULD SPEND WEEKENDS THERE. MY FAMLY LIFE AND MY TELEVISION LIFE WERE IN SEPARATE COMPARTMENTS AND NEVER COALESCED, EXCEPT FOR ONE INCIDENT.

ON A SATURDAY MORNING MY SON SAID HE WANTED TO TAKE ME TO SEE A NEW FILM, "SHOT IN THE DARK," TO SEE HOW HARD I COULD LAUGH." HE ASSURED ME THAT IT WAS A REALLY A GREAT MOVIE. HE WAS RIGHT. IT WAS A VERY FUNNY FILM. THE AUDIENCE ROARED WITH LAUGHTER. I JOINED THEM. STEPHEN WAS THANKED PROFUSELY FOR THE INVITE.

THE FOLLOWING MONDAY I WALKED INTO GRANT'S OFFICE AND TOLD HIM I'D SEEN A MOVIE THAT WOULD MAKE A GREAT SERIES. "IT'S ABOUT A CLUTZY DETECTIVE WHO CAN'T DO ANY THING RIGHT. IT'S HILARIOUS. YOU'VE GOT TO SEE IT."

GRANT AND HIS WIFE, MARY TYLER MOORE, SAW THE FILM A FEW NIGHTS LATER. THE NEXT MORNING HE CAME INTO MY OFFICE AND SAID, "YOU'RE RIGHT. LET'S GET MOVING ON IT."

LATE THAT AFTERNOON GRANT HAD A MEETING AT THE BEVERLY HILLS HOTEL. AS HE WAS WALKING UP THE ENTRY STEPS, MEL BROOKS WAS WALKING DOWN. GRANT TOLD ME ABOUT THEIR TWENTY-SECOND CONVERSATION. IT WENT SOMETHING LIKE THIS: GRANT, "HI, MEL. YOU LOOK UPSET. WHAT'S WRONG?"

MEL, "I JUST HAD A GREAT SCRPT TURNED DOWN BY ABC."

GRANT, "HAVE YOU GOT IT?"

MEL. "YEAH, RIGHT HERE."

GRANT, "GIVE IT TO ME."

MEL HANDED THE SCRIPT TO GRANT AND WALKED TO HIS CAR.

IN THE MORNING, GRANT CAME INTO MY OFFICE AND THREW A SCRIPT ON MY DESK AND SAID, "READ IT."

I READ IT, WENT INTO HIS OFFICE AND SAID, "IT'S SHOT IN THE DARK."

THAT IS HOW NBC GAINED A HIT SERIES CALLED, "GET SMART," STARRING DON ADAMS. IT RAN FROM NINETTEEN SIXTY-FIVE TO SIXTY-NINE. STEPHEN NEVER GOT THE CREDIT HE DESERVED.

CHAPTER

16

RICKI AND I HAD ONE VERY SPECIAL FRIEND, RUDI GERNREICH, THE FIRST BONA FIDE FASHION DESIGNER TO COME OUT OF THE CALIFORNIA YOUTH CULTURE OF THE SIXTIES. RUDI WAS A REBEL. HE OUTRAGED SOME PEOPLE WITH HIS TOPLESS BATHING SUIT, HIS SEE-THROUGH TOPS AND BRAS. HE SPENT MANY A WEEKEND WITH US. RICKI WOULD TRAVEL WITH HIM TO NEW YORK WHEN HE WENT THERE TO SHOW HIS NEW LINE OF DRESSES AND KNITWEAR TO BUYERS. AT THE PEAK OF HIS CAREER, I WAS VISITING HIM IN HIS WORK SPACE ON SANTA MONICA BLVD. ON ONE SIDE OF THE LARGE ROOM THERE WAS A RACK OF CLOTHES WITH A CLUSTER OF YOUNG WOMEN PAWING THROUGH THEM. I ASKED RUDI WHO THEY WERE AND WHAT THEY WERE THEY DOING. MAY, HIS ASSISTANT, ANSWERED THAT THEY WERE MODELS HERE TO BUY LAST SEASON'S UNSOLD GARMENTS. "WE WANT TO GET SOME OF OUR MONEY BACK, BUT THE GIRLS ARE A PAIN IN THE NECK, ALWAYS IN THE WAY."

I REMEMBER TURNING TO MAY TO ASK, "ARE THERE A LOT OF UNSOLDS EVERY SEASON?"

"SURE. WE OVER-CUT FOR ORDERS AND REORDERS."

I LOOKED OVER AT THE GIRLS AND NOTED THAT THERE WAS MORE THAN ONE RACK OF CLOTHES THAT THE GIRLS WERE PUSHING THROUGH. RUDI AND I TALKED FOR A LITTLE WHILE. I LEFT WITH AN IDEA SWIRLING AROUND IN MY HEAD. I TALKED TO RICKI ABOUT WHAT I'D WITNESSED THAT AFTERNOON. SHE TOLD ME THAT EVERY FASHION DESIGNER HAS THE SAME PROBLEM WITH OVER CUTS. THOUGH THEY ARE THE PREVIOUS SEASON'S PRODUCT, THEY CAN'T HAVE THEM SELLING AT CUT-RATE PRICES IN OFF-STREET, EASILY ACCESSED SHOPS.

NOW MY LITTLE GREY CELLS WERE SUPER CHARGED AND HERE IS WHY: THOSE GIRLS WERE THERE SEEKING BARGAINS, THEY KNEW THEY WERE BARGAINS BECAUSE OF RUDI'S REPUTATION AND MOST IMPORTANT THEY KNEW THE COST OF HIS CLOTHES IN THE SMART AND ELEGANT STORES AND SHOPS. I CONCENTRATED ON THOSE FACTS AND, RATHER QUICKLY, CONCEIVED A WAY TO "HELP" THOSE POOR, DESPERATE FASHION DESIGNERS.

WE HAD ANOTHER FRIEND, ARLEN GREENWOOD, WHO HAD BEEN IN AND AROUND THE FASHION BUSINESS FOR YEARS. WHEN MY CONCEPT WAS SPELLED OUT TO HER SHE WONDERED WHY SOMEONE HADN'T ALREADY TRIED TO PUT SOMETHING LIKE THIS TOGETHER. BUT, SHE SAID, "I'VE BEEN A SALES

PERSON. I'VE BEEN THERE AND DONE THAT AND I'M VERY GOOD AT IT AND DON'T WANT TO GO BACK TO IT."

I SAID,"ARLEN, THERE WILL BE NO 'SELLING.' YOU AND RICKI WILL MAKE PROFESSIONAL FASHION COMMENTS ABOUT A WOMAN'S CHOICES AND COLLECT HER MONEY." THE WOMEN COMING IN WILL BE PRESELECTED WITH REGARD TO THEIR FASHION SENSE AND THEIR KNOWLEDGE OF THE COSTS INVOLVED IN DRESSING IN HIGH FASHION GARMENTS. I WANT YOU AND RICKI TO BE PARTNERS IN OWNERSHIP AND THE SHARING OF PROFITS."

ARLEN WAS A SUPER SMART LADY. SHE LOOKED AT ME, SMILED AND SAID, "IF YOU CAN PUT THIS ALL TOGETHER, COUNT ME IN."

EVER SINCE RICKI LEFT NEW YORK AND HER EMINENT CAREER, I'D BEEN CONCERNED THAT SHE WAS DEMEANING HERSELF AS A HOUSEWIFE, THAT AT SOME POINT SHE MIGHT FEEL BITTER AND RESENTFUL. WE HAD AGREED THAT COSTLY OVERCUTS WERE A SIZABLE LOSS TO DESIGNERS. I POINTED OUT THAT PEOPLE LOVED A BARGAIN IF THEY KNEW FOR SURE IT WAS TRULY A GOOD DEAL. I THEN OUTLINED FOR HER A WAY TO BRING RUDI'S LOSS ITEMS, AT BARGAIN PRICES, TO THE PUBLIC. WE'LL RID HIM OF HIS PESKY VISITORS BY SELLING HIS DRESSES IN THE MOST SHIELDING MANNER POSSIBLE AT HIS COST WITH A SPLIT OF TWO-THIRDS TO HIM AND ONE-THIRD TO US ON A CONSISIGNMENT BASIS. WE'LL RENT OFFICE SPACE SOME WHERE ON VENTURA BLVD, PREFERABLY IN ENCINO. ARLIN WILL BECOME A PARTNER AND ON A SOLID, NO LOOK-THROUGH, GLASS, DOOR THERE WILL BE A CHIC, SMALL PLAQUE THAT READS, "VANDUSEN GREEN." NO ONE WILL GET PAST THAT DOOR WITHOUT AN APPOINTMENT. YOU AND ARLEN WILL MAKE CONTACT WITH WOMEN WHO ARE IN TELEVISION OR FEATURE FILMS AND WE WILL MAKE A TEST RUN WITH RUDI'S THINGS AND IF EVERTHING WORKS WE'LL MAKE CONTACT WITH OTHER WELL KNOWN SOUTHERN CALIFORNIA DESIGNERS AND OFFER THEM THE SAME ARRANGEMENT AS RUDI'S.

WE HAD DINNER WITH RUDI, I EXPLAINED MY PLAN, AND HE AGREED ENTHUSIASTICALLY.

A YEAR LATER IN ENCINO THERE WAS BLACK DOOR WITH A CHIC PLAQUE. BEHIND THE DOOR THERE WERE THREE ROOMS, ONE A GOOD SIZE. THE ONLY EMBELLISHMENTS TO THE BARE WALLS WERE WHEELED RACKS LOADED WITH WOMEN'S CLOTHING BY MOST OF CALIFORNIA AND NEW YORK HIGH FASHION DESIGNERS. (I HAD SENT THE TWO LADIES BACK EAST TO EXPLAIN HOW VANDUSEN GREEN REPRESENTED THE CALIFORNIA DESIGNERS AND TO OFFER THE SAME ARRANGEMENT TO THE FASHION MAVINS THERE. THEY HAD BEEN REMARKABLY SUCCESSFUL ON THEIR THREE DAY MISSION.) THE ROOMS WERE CLEAN, BUT THERE WAS NO INVITING DÉCOR, NO PLACES TO SIT AND LOUNGE, NO PRIVACY, ONLY ONE MIRROR, A SMALL DESK FOR TRANSACTIONS AND TWO LADIES WHO KNEW WHAT THEY WERE TALKING ABOUT WHEN DICUSSING FASHION AND ITS TRENDS. WHEN JENNIFER JONES, AN ACADEMY AWARD WINNER, SENT HER CHAUFFEUR TO PICKUP TEN DRESSES SO SHE COULD SELECT FOUR WE KNEW, CONVINCINGLY, THAT EVERYBODY AND THAT MEANS EVERBODY LOVES A BARGAIN. AND THAT WE HAD A WINNER !N VANDUSEN GREEN THAT BECAME A REAITY BECAUSE OF MY WITNESSING YOUNG LADIES PULL DRESSES OFF WHEELED RACKS. THE HAPPENING BECAME AN EVENT THAT BROUGHT MAJOR LIFE-CHANGES TO RICKI AND ME.

CHAPTER

17

VANDUSEN GREEN WAS A SUCCESS BY ANY STANDARD. WORD OF MOUTH OF HIGH FASHION AT BARGAIN PRICES SPREAD LIKE WILD FIRE. THOSE WHO KNEW FASHION AND ITS PRICES CALLED FOR APPOINTMENTS. VANDUSEN GREEN NO LONGER DEPENDED ON TELEVISION AND THE MOTION PICTURE INDUSTRY FOR CUSTOMERS

I HAD SPENT A MORNING IN MY NBC OFFICE THAT RAN LONG BECAUSE OF A SERIES OF LENGTHY MEETINGS. BEFORE DRIVING BACK TO PARAMOUT, I DECIDED TO HAVE A LATE LUNCH AT ALFONSES' IN TOLUCA LAKE. IT WAS STILL CROWDED AND I SAT AT THE PIANO BAR NEXT TO A PAIR OF LADIES TALKING ABOUT VANDUSEN GREEN. ONE HAD BEEN THERE AND WAS DESCRIBING, RATHER PROULY, HOW THIS VERY SPECIAL BOUTIQUE OPERATED. SHE DETAILED VANDUSEN GREEN JUST AS I HAD CONCIEVED IT. IT WAS LIKE LISTENING TO A PLAYBACK OF ONE OF MY EARLY PRESENTATIONS. IT WAS ENOUGH FOR ME TO HEAR HER TELLING A FRIEND OF THE WONDERS OF OUR SHOP. I DID NOT INTRODUCE MYSELF, THOUGH IT WAS TEMPTING.

RICKI HAD HER NEW AND FLOURISHING BUSINESS. I WAS BUSY SHOOTING PILOTS FOR NBC PRODUCTIONS AND WE WERE LIVING IN A MODERN, ELEGANTLY LANDSCAPED, NEW HOUSE HIGH ABOVE THE VALLEY WITH A SPECTACULAR 180 DEGEE VIEW. I THOUGHT WE WERE BOTH HAPPY BEING BUSY, HEALTHY AND PRODUCTIVE. THE KIDS WERE OLDER, MORE SELF-DETERMINING AND LESS DEMANDING OF OUR TIME. WE HAD BEEN TOGETHER A LONG TIME WITHOUT MAJOR PROBLEMS TO DISTURB OR DISRUPT US.

ONE DAY WHILE HAVING LUNCH AT MONTY'S, A RESTAURANT ACROSS VENTURA BLVD. FROM VANDUSEN GREEN, OUT OF THE BLUE, RICKI SAID THAT I HAD OUTGROWN HER AND SHE WANTED A DIVORCE. AFTER THAT STUPEFYING, DEVESTATING AND BAFFLING STATEMENT I FELT AS IF I HAD BEEN STABBED THROUGH MY HEART INTO THE DEEPEST RECESSES OF MY SOUL. I COULDN'T HAVE BEEN MORE SURPRISED IF SHE FLAPPED HER ARMS AND FLOWN AROUND THE ROOM. WHAT WAS SAID IS UNCLEAR, BUT OUR "CONVERSATION" MUST HAVE GONE SOMETHING LIKE THIS:

I SURELY ASKED, "OUTGROWN?"

RICKI: "YOU ARE NOW THE HEAD OF NBC PRODUCTIONS," AS IF THAT WAS ALL THAT NEEDED TO BE SAID.

"I WASN'T MADE HEAD OF MGM OR WARNER BROTHERS. NBC PRODUCTIONS PRODUCES TELEVISION SHOWS NOT MILLION-DOLLAR MOVIES. I'LL BE DOING ESSENTIALLY WHAT I'VE BEEN DOING FOR THE PAST TWO OR THREE YEARS."

HER REFUSAL TO ACCEPT MY NEW POSITION AS A GOOD THING FOR BOTH OF US WAS ASTONISHING. I DIDN'T KNOW WHAT MORE TO SAY. IT WAS MIND-BOGGLING TO TRY AND RELATE DIVORCE WITH WHAT I THOUGHT WAS NOT A BAD BUT EXCELENT MARRIAGE. WANTING A DIVORCE WAS SUCH A STARTLING, CALCULATED DECISION, IT HURT TO BE SO COLDLY REJECTED AFTER A SHARED LIFE OF GOOD FORTUNE THAT BROUGHT UNFORESEEN ACCOMPLISHMENTS. I ASKED FOR TIME TO THINK ABOUT HER SURPRISING REQUEST. I DIDN'T HAVE CLUE AS TO WHY SHE WANTED A DIVORCE, BUT I KNEW THE REASON GIVEN WAS TOO IRRATIONAL TO BE BELIEVED.

WE TALKED A LOT AT DIFFERENT TIMES. I PLEADED WITH HER TO CHANGE HER MIND BUT SHE REMAINED ADAMENT. PROCEEDINGS BEGAN AND ENDED AGREEABLY. I CHOSE NOT TO BE PRESENT IN COURT SO I DIDN'T KNOW, OR CARED TO KNOW, WHAT RICKI'S RATIONALE WAS TO GAIN THE FINAL DECREE. THERE WAS THE USUAL CALIFORNIA SPLITTING OF ASSETS, EXCEPT FOR MY GIVING VANDUSEN GREEN TO RICKI WITH THE STIPULATION THAT IF HER INCOME FROM THE BUSINESS EVER EXCEEDED MINE I WOULD NO LONGER PAY ALIMONY. I DON'T KNOW WHY I DID THAT. NEVERTHELESS, IT PROVED TO BE A VERY WISE MOVE.

CHAPTER

18

MY SEEING THOSE YOUNG GIRLS GOING THROUGH RUDI'S OVERCUTS WAS IMPORTANT. IT HELPED ME FORMULATE A CONCEPT THAT MADE VANDUSEN GREEN A REALITY. THEN VANDUSEN GREEN AND ITS LIFE TRANSFORMING SUCCESS THAT SOMEHOW MADE RICKI SECURE ENOUGH TO DIVORCE ME. THE DIVORCE WAS PAINFUL, BUT WHEN THINGS ARE MOST BLEAK THEY CAN PROVE TO BE BENEFICIAL AS THEY LUCKILY DID FOR ME.

I MOVED INTO A BEATIFULLY FURNISHED APARTMENT AT OLIVE AND THE SUNSET STRIP. MY DAYS WERE FILLED WITH THE PROBLEMS INHERENT TO A PRODUCTION COMPANY, BUT MY INTEREST IN PRODUCTION ENTANGLEMENTS LESSENED. MY NIGHTS WERE HARD TO HANDLE. THEY WERE DIRECTIONLESS, WITHOUT MEANING. THERE WERE NO ATTACHMENTS, NOR ANY PLACE I NEEDED TO BE. I HAD LOST EVERYTHING I'D CARED ADOUT, MAYBE EVEN THE ABILITY TO TRUST AND LOVE AGAIN.

I WALKED THE LENGTH OF THE STRIP ALMOST EVERY NIGHT, GO IN TO ONE OF ITS FINE RESTAURANTS, SIT AT THE BAR, HAVE A DRINK AND THEN HAVE DINNER. USUALLY, I WOULD PAY NO ATTENTION TO THE PEOPLE OR THE SURROUNDING CHATTER.

ONE NIGHT SITTING AT THE BAR IN FRASCOTTI'S TWO WOMEN CAME IN AND SAT NEXT TO ME ON STOOLS JUST VACATED. ONE WAS VERY DRUNK AND AFTER THEIR DRINKS WERE SERVED THE OTHER LADY WAS SAYING OVER AND OVER, "YOU PROMISED ME AFTER ONE DRINK, YOU'D LET ME TAKE YOU HOME." THERE WAS DESPERATION IN HER VOICE. I LEANED TOWARD HER AND WHISPERED, "CAN I HELP?"

SHE WHISPERED BACK, "YOU CAN TRY."

WE DID, FINALLY, GET MS. DRUNK INTO THE SOBER LADY'S CAR AND I RODE ALONG TO HELP GET HER INTO HER HOUSE IN BEVERLY HILLS. ONCE SHE WAS ASLEEP ON HER COUCH, MS. GOOD SAMARTAN SAID, AS WE WERE LEAVING, "THANKS FOR YOUR HELP. I DON'T KNOW WHAT I WOULD HAVE DONE WITH HER. SHE'S A WELL KNOWN DECORATOR WHO COMES IN TO THE IMPORT HOUSE I MANAGE. SHE DRINKS, OBVIOUSLY. I'LL TAKE YOU BACK TO YOUR CAR. BY THE WAY, MY NAME IS SUE MCKAY."

I SAID, "I WALKED TO THE RESTAURANT SO I DON'T HAVE A CAR. I'M JOHN HINSEY." SHE LOOKED AT ME AND WITH A LAUGH SAID, "OKAY, JOHN. IF THAT'S HOW IT IS, I'LL DRIVE YOU HOME."

I ASKED, "HAVE YOU EATEN?"

"NO."

"INSTEAD OF TAKING ME HOME WHY DON'T WE GO BACK AND HAVE DINNER? I'M HUNGRY AND REALLY WOULD NOT LIKE TO EAT ALONE TONIGHT."

SHE LOOKED AT ME AND WHILE SMILING SAID, "IS HELPING A LADY GET A DRUNKEN LADY HOME YOUR MODUS OPERADI FOR GETTING A DINNER COMPANION?"

"NEVER TRIED IT BEFORE IF IT WORKS, IT WILL BE."

"IT WORKED. LET'S HAVE DINNER."

THAT IS VERY CLOSE TO HOW SUE AND I MET, AT JUST THE RIGHT TIME.

AS WE WENT INTO FRASCATTI'S, I ASKED IF SHE'D LIKE A DRINK BEFORE WE WERE SEATED. SHE SAID, NOT AT THAT BAR, ONCE IS ENOUGH FOR ME TONIGHT. WHILE A TABLE WAS BEING CLEARED, SUE TOLD ME A LITTLE ABOUT "HELEN:" SHE'S TALENTED, LONELY AFTER HER RECENT DIVORCE AND TRIES TO DRINK AWAY THE ALONENESS. SHE EXPLAINED THAT SHE'D ARRIVED AT ALPINE, THE IMPORT HOUSE, ALREADY SOUSED AND THAT SHE HAD GOTTEN HER OUT BY PROMISING HER A DRINK AND THAT I KNEW THE REST OF THE SAD TALE.

WE WERE SEATED AND I HAD A CHANCE TO STUDY THE WOMEN ACROSS FROM ME AS SHE LOOKED AT THE MENU. SHE WAS ATTRACTIVE, WELL DRESSED AND HER HANDS WERE LOVELY WITH ONLY A CLEAR POLISH ON HER PERFECTLY MANICURED NAILS. I NOTICED TOO THAT THERE WAS NO WEDDING RING.

WE TALKED EASILY AND COMFORTABLY. SHE TOLD ME SHE HAD LIVED IN SAN FRANCISCO, HAD A HOME IN MILL VALLEY COMPLETE WITH HUSBAND AND HOLDING UP HER LEFT HAND SAID, "BOTH ARE STILL THERE AND I'M HERE BECAUSE THE MARRIAGE TURNED SOUR, AND I DID NOT WANT TO GO TO CHICAGO." THAT COMMENT ABOUT CHICAGO PUZZLED ME, BUT I LET IT GO. SHE LOOKED SAD FOR MOMENT AND THEN SAID, BRIGHTLY, "I MISS THE GOLDEN GATE BRIDGE AND THE CABLE CARS."

I ASKED IF SHE WAS DIVORCED AND SHE SAID, "IN THE PROCESS." SHE HESITATED AND THEN ASKED, "WHAT ABOUT YOU, WHY ARE YOU WALKING THE STRIP AND SITTING AT A BAR ALONE? YOU DON'T LOOK LIKE A PERSON WHO ENJOYS SITTING AT A BAR OR BEING ALONE." AGAIN, THERE WAS THAT NICE SMILE.

"I DON'T," I SAID. "I SIT AT THE BAR TO HAVE A WELL DESERVED DRINK BEFORE HAVING DINNER. LIKE YOU, I'M IN THE PROCESS."

SHE PAUSED AND SAID QUIETLY, "SORRY. IT'S A DIFFICULT TIME ISN'T IT?"

I NODDED.

WE HAD EATEN OUR SALADS DURING THAT EXCHANGE AND WHEN OUR ENTRE WAS SERVED THERE WAS NO MORE TALK OF DIVORCES. WE TALKED ABOUT SAN FRANCISCO AND "THE PAINTED LADIES," THE RENOWN, BEAUTIFULLY MAINTAINED VICTORNIAN HOUSES, ABOUT FLOWERY AND CURVY LOMBARD STREET, ABOUT GUMPS FOR EXPENSIVE SHOPPING AND THE MANY EXCELENT RESTAURANTS. I TOLD HER ABOUT NBC PRODUCTIONS AND MY PART IN THE ORGANIZATION. SHE DIDN'T EVIDENCE ANY INTEREST IN THE SHOOTING OF PILOTS, SO WE DISCUSSED HEAVY THINGS LIKE VEITNAM AND CIVIL RIGHTS.

THERE HAD BEEN DINNER OR DRINKS WTH A NUMBER OF WOMEN SINCE LEAVING "HOME." NOT ONE OF THOSE ENCOUNTERS INTERESTED ME, I WAS HAPPY TO SAY GOODNIGHT. NOT THIS NIGHT. I WAS WITH AN INTELLEGENT, SELF-SUFFICIENT, CAPTIVATING, NONSHOW-BIZ WOMAN WHO WAS GOING TO REVERSE OUR ROLES BY TAKING ME TO MY APARTMENT. SHE SURPRISED AND PLEASED ME, ESPECIALLY, WHEN SHE GAVE ME HER PHONE NUMBER WITHOUT MY ASKING AND SAYING, "LET'S DO THIS AGAIN MINUS HELEN, OF COURSE."

WHEN WE PULLED UP IN FRONT OF THE FRENCH HILL SHE SAID, "SO THIS IS WHERE YOU'RE STAYING. I KNOW OF ITS UNIQUE UNITS, EACH ONE DIFFERENT, ALL DECORATED BY TOM DAWSON THE OWNER. I KNOW HIM FROM HIS COMING INTO THE ALPINE SHOW ROOM, NICE MAN ALWAYS COURTIOUS AND POLITE."

I WANTED DESPERATELY TO INVITE HER IN FOR FINAL CUP OF COFFEE. FEARFUL OF HER SEEING THE INVITATION AS A NOT SO CLEVER GAMBIT, I SAID, "I ENJOYED OUR EVENING TOGETHER. AND WOULD LIKE TO CALL AND DO IT AGAIN." WE SHOOK HANDS AND I SAID GOODNIGHT.

LAUGHING, SHE SAID, "SO CALL, JOHN HINSEY," AND DROVE OFF.

LOOKING BACK I SEE THAT IF SUE HAD DRIVEN HELEN DIRECTLY HOME, HAD NOT STOPPED FOR A FINAL DRINK AT FRASCOTTIS POPULAR BAR AND RETAURANT, AND THE TWO PEOPLE NEXT TO ME WERE NOT LEAVING AS THEY ENTERED, SUE AND I WOULD NEVER HAVE MET AND OUR FUTURES WOULD HAVE BEEN UNCERTAIN. THAT NIGHT DID I HAVE A GUARDIAN ANGEL WATCHING OVER ME? AND IF I DID: WHY? WHY WOULD I BE SUDDENLY SO SPECIAL, SO DESERVING? WHY COULDN'T IT BE JUST SOMETHING CONSEQUENTIAL CHANGING THE COURSE OF MY LIFE? OR WHY COULDN'T IT BE SIMPLY GOOD FORTUNE? INSTEAD, IT WAS ANOTHER LIFE- CHANGING EVENT THAT SET SUE AND ME ON A LIFE-FULFILLING JOURNEY THAT HAS SO FAR LASTED HALF A CNTURY. MAYBE AS I CONTINUE LOOKING BACK I'LL FIND SOME ANSWERS.

CHAPTER

19

THERE WAS A LONG TWO DAY WAIT BEFORE CALLING FOR A PROPER DATE. SHE ACCEPT AND ASKED WHAT SHE SHOULD WEAR?

"BASIC BLACK AND PEARLS IS ALWAYS APPROPRIATE."

"NO PROBLEM. WOULD YOU LIKE MY ADDRESS SO I CAN MAKE USE OF MY PEARLS? I LIVE ON LARABEE DO YOU KNOW WHERE THAT IS?"

"NEAR ME, BUT IT'S TO THE WEST, RIGHT?"

"YES, THAT'S RIGHT." SHE GAVE THE ADDRESS.

"SEVEN O'CLOCK?"

"SEVEN IS GOOD."

SUE HAD A VERY NICE, FIRST FLOOR APARTMENT. IN SHORT ORDER WE WERE ON OUR WAY TO CHASEN'S IN WEST HOLLYWOOD. SHE HADN'T BEEN THE LEAST BIT IMPRESSED BY MY SHOOTING PILOTS FOR TV, BUT, I THOUGHT, SHE MIGHT BE BY MY TAKING HER TO WHERE MOTION PICTURE AND TELEVISION LUMINARIES DINE. MAYBE I WOULD SEE SOMEBODY I KNEW AND SAY HELLO. AS WE WALKED IN SUE SAID, "I HAVEN'T HAD THEIR STEAK TARTARE IN A WHILE, THIS WILL BE A TREAT." FORGET ABOUT BEING IMPRESSED BY THE FAMOUS CHASEN'S. I DIDN'T SEE ANYBODY I KNEW!

WE TALKED LIKE VERY OLD FRIENDS. EACH LISTENED AND THEN MAKING A RELATED COMMENT. WHEN SHE HAD FINISHED HER STEAK TARTARE AND HAD REFUSED ANYTHING MORE, SHE SAID, "I'M DYING TO SEE ONE OF TOM DAWSON'S TASTEFUL APARTMENTS. YOU DO HAVE A STATE OF THE ART COFFEE MAKER, DON'T YOU?"

I SAID, "I DON'T KNOW ABOUT STATE OF THE ART, BUT I DO GRIND MY OWN BEANS. DOES THAT COUNT?"

"IT HELPS. CAN WE GO?"

AT THE FRENCH HILL, I PARKED IN MY DESIGNATED SPACE AND WE WALKED UP THE STAIRCASE TO MY DOOR. INSIDE, SUE WALKED AROUND, REMARKING ABOUT THE NUMBER OF ANTIQUES THERE WERE. OBVIOUSLY, LIKING WHAT SHE SAW.

I WENT INTO THE KITCHEN TO PREPARE THE COFFEE AND WHEN I RETURNED SHE WAS SITTING COMFORTABLY IN ONE OF THE CHAIRS AND SAID, WITHOUT ANY PREAMBLE, "I DON'T WANT YOU TO MISINTERPET MY WANTING TO COME HERE. I DID WANT TO SEE THE APARTMENT, HOWEVER, I DO NOT WANT TO START A RELATIONSHIP, I AM NOT READY FOR THAT. I HAVE SOME THINGS TO RESOLVE BEFORE THAT CAN HAPPEN. I LIKE YOU, JOHN, AND I AM ATTRACTED, BUT IT'S TOO SOON. DO YOU UNDERSTAND THAT?"

I COULDN'T HELP BUT LAUGH AND SAY, "YOU HAVE NO IDEA HOW RELIEVED I AM. I WAS WORRIED ABOUT WHAT TO DO NEXT. I'M ALSO ATTRACTED, BUT FAR FROM READY FOR A SERIOUS RELATIONSHIP. I'M MORE THAN READY FOR AN INTERESTING FRIEND TO SIT ACROSS FROM ME AT A FINE RESTAURANT AND TALK AND LAUGH. I WOULD APPRECIATE YOUR DINING WITH ME MORE THAN JUST NOW AND THEN. CAN WE AGREE TO DO THAT?"

WITH THAT GREAT SMILE SHE SAID, "IT'S AN ACCEPTABLE ARRANGEMENT."

SHE PUT DOWN HER EMPTY CUP. WE SHOOK HANDS AGAIN, AS IF WE'D CLOSED AN IMPORTANT BUSINESS DEAL. SHE SAID, "TOMORROW IS A BUSY DAY, WOULD YOU TAKE ME HOME PLEASE."

SUE AND I WERE TOGETHER MOST EVENINGS. WE BOTH LOVED GOOD FOOD, SO WE HAD DINNER IN RESTAURANTS FROM WHERE THE ROSE BOWL PARADE IS HOSTED TO WHERE THE AFFLUENT LIVE IN BEACHFRONT ENCLAVES. ONE SATURDAY SHE WAS INTRODUCED TO MY DAUTGHTER, DARRAGH, A SOPHISTICATE AT SIXTEEN, AND MY CONTRIBUTION TO THE EVENING WAS THAT OF A GOOD AND PATIENT LISTENER.

UNDETERRED BY OUR RESOLVES TO AVOID A RELATIONSHIP, WE FELL DEEPLY AND PASSIONATELY IN LOVE. OUR PRIVATE MOMENTS WERE A SHARED INTIMACY THE LIKE OF WHICH I HAD NEVER DREAMED OR EXPERIENCED. I DON'T THINK EITHER ONE OF US THOUGHT THAT WE COULD BE SO INVOLVED AGAIN, ESPECIALLY SO SOON AFTER EACH OF US SUFFERED A DIVORCE. ONCE WE ACCEPTED OUR NEED TO BE MORE THAN JUST FRIENDS, THE REST WAS EASY. HAVING TWO APARTMENTS WAS UTTERLY AND PATHETICALLY STUPID, SO SHE MOVED INTO MINE. NO PROBLEM THERE, THIS WAS THE 60'S WHEN CHANGE, EXPERIMENTATION, AND QUESTIONING TRADITIONAL MORES WERE THE MODES OF THE DAY. WE WERE SIMPLY A PART OF A NEW CULTURE AND LOVING IT. WE WELCOMED WHAT IS, AND LOOKED FORWARD TO WHAT WILL BE.

CHAPTER

20

I SOMETIMES WONDER WHAT MY LIFE WOULD HAVE BEEN LIKE IF SUE AND I HADN'T TAKEN ON THE ROLES OF GOOD SAMARITANS THAT NIGHT IN FRASCATTI'S BAR. TWO PEOPLE WITH DIIFFERENT BACKGROUNDS, DIFFERENT LIFE STYLES BY CHANCE MEET IN A CERTAIN PLACE AT A CERTAIN TIME AND THEIR LIVES TAKE ON AN ENTIRELY DIFFERENT COURSE THAT LASTS THE REST OF THEIR LIVES. WE MAY NEVER HAVE BEEN AWARE OF EACH OTHER'S EXISTENCE AND EACH OF US WOULD HAVE CONTINUED ON IN A DIRECTION UNTESTED AND UNKNOWN.

SUE, TO ME, WAS THE SUMMA CUM LAUDE GRADUATE OF A SCHOOL THAT TAUGHT ITS STUDENTS TO ENJOY LIFE TO THE FULLEST, TO SHAPE THEIR OWN GOALS AND AMBITIONS, TO NOT HOLD BACK ON ANY HONEST EXPRESSION OF EMOTION. SHE WAS UNLIKE ANYONE I'D EVER KNOWN. LOOKING BACK, I SEE THAT SUE, METAPHORICALLY, WAS A TELL-ALL BOOK. SHE AWAKENED ME TO A WIDE AND WONDEROUS NEW WORLD.

RICKI IS A BEAUTIFUL WOMAN AND I LOVED HER JUST AS I LOVED AN EXQUISTE PIECE OF MUSEUM ART. METAPHORICALLY, SHE IS NOT YET A BOOK, SHE IS THE BEGINNING OF A MANUSCRIPT MADE UNTIDY BY MARGINALIA, CROSSOUTS AND ADDITIONS. ANYONE ATTEMPTING TO WRITE HER BIOGRAPHY WOULD HAVE FOUND HER DIFFICULT TO PIN DOWN. AFTER TWENTY-TWO YEARS, I DIDN'T KNOW WHETHER OR NOT SHE HAD UNSHAKABLE OPINIONS. EVERYONE LOVED HER BECAUSE THERE WAS NOTHING IN HER ATTITUDE TO DISLIKE. WE NEVER ARGUED BECAUSE WE NEVER DISAGREED. WE NEVER HAD DISCUSSIONS ABOUT THE LATEST BEST SELLER BECAUSE I NEVER SAW WITH A BOOK. SHE ONLY WATCHED TELEVISION IF I TURNED IT ON. SHE SEEMED CONTENT AND WAS ALWAYS WILLING TO DO WHAT I SUGGESTED. I REALIZE NOW THAT I MISSED LIVING WITH A PERSON WHO HAD DEEP SEATED LIKES AND DISLIKES TO ENLIVEN A DULL SUNDAY. SOMETIMES HER NONREACTIONS TO SITUATIONS CONFUSED ME, BUT I'D CARRY ON AS IF IT DIDN'T MATTER. MOST WOMEN, IT'S GENERALIZED, THINK FIRST WITH THEIR HEARTS, THEN WITH THEIR HEADS. RICKI DID NEITHER, A LAIS SEZ FAIRE ATTITUDE SAVED HER FROM HAVING TO THINK AT ALL.

WHEN RICKI AND I MET, SHE WAS EIGHTEEN AND I WAS TWENTY-TWO. NEITHER OF US COULD LOOK FOREWARD TO ANYTHING OTHER THAN THE WAR TO END. I REMEMBER HER SAYING WHEN WE WERE TOGTHER IN SAN FRANCISCO, "I'M NOT WORRIED ABOUT THE FUTURE YOU'LL TAKE CARE OF ME." THE EARNESTLY DELIVERED COMMENT SHOCKED ME. I HADN'T GOTTEN MARRIED TO BE A CAREGIVER, BUT

TO SHARE A LIFE, BUILD A FUTURE TOGETHER. I FINALLY DISMISSED IT AS AN INNOCENT DECLARATION OF THE UTMOST TRUST AND LOVE.

WHEN THE COSTLY WAR DID END, I WAS HAPPY, BUT LOST. I HADN'T THE SLIGHTEST NOTION OF HOW TO BEGIN SECURING A FUTURE. I HAD NEVER KNOWN WHERE I WAS GOING OR WHY. HINDSIGHT REMINDS ME THAT SO FAR I HAD LIVED ACCEPTING WHAT LIFE AND EVENTS HAD DELIVERED. I BECAME, THROUGHOUT OUR MARRIAGE THE DECISION MAKER. UNINTENTIONALLY, MY DECISION TO LEAVE HOLLYWOOD AND GO TO NEW YORK CHANGED HER LIFE, AND MINE, FOR THE REST OF OUR TIME TOGETHER AND BEYOND.

AFTER SIGHTSEEING, WHEN RICKI MET JOAN WEBSTER AT SOCIETY OF MODELS, A FAST MOVING PROCESS BEGAN WITH AN ENDING THAT WE WEREN'T PREPARED FOR OR LUSTED AFTER. THE WHOLE OF HER NEW YORK EXPERIENCE FROM ARRIVAL TO BECOMING AN ESTABLISHED HIGH FASHION MODEL WAS MIND BLOWING. HER EASY ACCEPTANCE OF WHAT HAD HAPPENED WAS PUZZELING. NOT IN ANY WAY DID SHE DEMONSTRATE THAT SHE WAS PLEASED, SURPRISED OR ASTONISHED BY WHAT HAD TAKEN PLACE. I FOUND IT OVERWHELMING.

RICKI HAD BECOME AN INTEGRAL PART OF A HIGHLY EXCLUSIVE GROUPING OF INTELLEGENT AND TALENTED PEOPLE AND WAS UNIMPRESSED. THAT SHOULD HAVE CONFUSED ME. I DIDN'T WONDER WHY SHE HADN'T REACTED IN THE TIME-HONORED WAY TO AN UNEXPECTED GIFT OF SUCH PROPORTIONS.

MY DECISION TO TAKE ADVANTAGE OF A SITUATION FACING ALL ENTREPRENEURS OF FASHION BY CONCEIVING AND ESTABLISHING VANDUSEN GREEN GAVE RICKI ANOTHER CHANCE TO ACQUIRE AN ENVIABLE POSITION OF STATUS WITH ONE MAJOR ALTERATION. THIS TIME SHE WAS NOT REQUIRED TO PLEASE OR SERVE OTHER PEOPLE. SHE HAD BECOME AN AUTHORITY FIGURE. SHE COULD MAKE DECISIONS, BUT ONLY WITHIN THE CONFINES OF VANDUSEN GREEN.

HER FIRST AND ONLY DECISION OF CONSEQUENCE, THAT I'M AWARE OF, WAS DIVORCING ME. I DIDN'T KNOW WHY A DIVORCE WHEN EVERYTHING SEEMED TO BE GOING SO WELL. I PONDERED, BUT DIDN'T COME WITH SATISFACTORY ANSWER EXCEPT THAT THE DIVORCE OCCURRED AND SUE AND I MET AND CREATED A SOLID RELATIONSHIP FOR WHICH I'M GRATEFUL.

FOR NOW, BACK TO RICKI: SHE WANTED ME TO TAKE CARE OF HER, AND I DID WILLINGLY. I MADE IT POSSIBLE FOR HER TO AVOID ANONYMITY, TO LIVE AND SUCCEED IN PULSATING, OFTEN CRUEL BUT FORGIVING NEW YORK CITY. TO MEET AND BECOME FRIENDS WITH TALENTED PEOPLE WHO WERE OUTSIDE OF SELF-CENTERED HOLLYWOOD. ALL OF THAT ENDED BY FEEDING A BOGUS SENSE OF SELF-WORTH THAT JUSTIFIED DEMANDING A DIVORCE, MY PAYING UNNEEDED ALIMONY AND TO HAVING MY ATTORNEY AGREE WITH ALL OF HER MINOR SETTLEMENT STIPULATIONS.

REVIEWING ALL OF THAT, I THINK I UNDERSTAND MY NOT HAVING RECEIVED AT LEAST A SINGLE OBLIGITORY THANK YOU.

RICKI IS A GENETICALLY ENHANCED WOMAN WHO GOT LUCKY. SHE DIDN'T ACHIEVE RECOGNITION AND RESPECT THROUGH HER OWN INITATIVE AND HARD WORK. SHE, THEREFORE, MUST NOT HAVE HAD AN

INNMOST PRIDE FOR HER ACHIEVEMENTS, WHICH, I BELIEVE, LEFT HER UNABLE TO SUSTAIN THE SELF-IMPOSED SWITCH TO MAKING DECISIONS ON HER OWN.

I WILL FORGIVE HER FOR DIVORCING ME AND FORCING ME TO TAKE ON THE PERVERSE BURDEN OF CONTIUING TO KEEP ON LIVING WHILE FACING A VAGUE FUTURE BECAUSE I WILL BE FOREVER INDEBTED THAT SHE INADVERTENTLY MADE IT POSSIBLE FOR ME TO MEET SUE AND FIND AN UNPREDICTABLE CONTENTMENT.

SUE, TOO, HAD A CAREER, THOUGH ONE UNHERALDED. SHE HAD BEEN AN EXECUTIVE ASSISTANT TO DR. MORTIMER J. ADLER, THE LAUDED PHILOSOPHER AND ASSOCIATE EDITOR OF THE "GREAT BOOKS OF THE WESTERN WORLD." SHE, BECAUSE OF HER ABILITIES, HAD SECURED THAT POSITION ON HER OWN. NO ONE COULD HAVE PAVED THE WAY TO A JOB WITH SUCH SCOPE AND SO MANY DUTIES THAT OFTEN HAD HER ON TWA'S SLEEPER FLIGHTS TO EUROPE AND MAJOR CITIES HERE IN THE STATES. SHE WAS A DECISIVE WOMAN, INTERESTING AND PROVATIVE AND I LOVED HER BECAUSE WHEN WE DISAGREED WE TOOK SIDES AND WON POINTS OR LOST POINTS DEPENDING ON OUR ABILITY TO DEBATE CALMLY AND WITH PURPOSE, BUT THEN JUST AS CALMLY ACKNOWLEDGE. HONOR AND RESPECT THE WINNER OF WHATEVER THE DISPUTE WAS ABOUT.

BACK TO TELEVISION:

CHAPTER

21

WE WERE READY TO SHOOT THE THREE PILOTS AT PARAMOUNT STUDIOS T.H.E. CAT WAS FIRST ON THE SCHEDULE. I SPENT A WEEK IN SAN FRANCISCO WHERE THE FIRST SHOOTING TOOK PLACE. IN A RENTED PROJECTION ROOM BORIS SEGAL'S PREVIOUS DAY'S WORK LOOKED GREAT. HE HAD SOME NIGHT SHOTS THAT WERE SENSATIONAL. THINGS WERE LOOKING GOOD.

WE RETURNED TO PARAMOUNT STUDIOS WHERE BORIS SHOT SOME INTERIORS, AND THEN BEGAN TO EDIT "CAT." I ATTENDED PREPRODUCTION MEETINGS FOR THE SHOOTING OF BILL BLATTY'S PLOTKIN PRISON. BILL, ALSO IN THE MIDST OF A DIVORCE, AND I HAD BECOME FAST FRIENDS. HE WOULD JOIN SUE AND ME FOR DINNER FREQUENTLY.

ONE NIGHT HE ASKED, NONCHALANTLY, DO EITHER OF YOU BELIEVE IN EXORCISM? IT SEEMED LIKE SUCH A STRANGE QUESTION THAT WE BOTH HESITATED ANSWERING. WE SHRUGGED AND SAID SOMETHING THAT INDICATED WE WEREN'T SURE. I DON'T KNOW IF HE WANTED TO EXCHANGE VIEWS ON THE SUBJECT OR NOT, BUT HE DROPPED IT AFTER OUR DEMURRING RESPONSE. I DO KNOW, TODAY, THAT AT THE TIME HE WAS WRITING HIS FUTURE BEST SELLER, "THE EXOCIST," AND WOULD LATER WRITE THE SCREENPLAY THAT WON AN ACADEMY AWARD. IT'S TOO BAD THAT WE FAILED TO ENCOURAGE FURTHER DISCUSSION. WHAT AN EXCEPTIONAL DINNER THAT COULD HAVE BEEN.

THROUGHOUT THE SHOOTING OF "PLOTKIN," I WAS CONCERNED ABOUT THE DIRECTOR'S APPROACH TO THE MATERIAL. OUR STAR, DON RICKLES, APPEARED TO BE HAPPY AND UNTROUBLED. HE WAS A DREAM ON THE SET, FUN AND COOPERTIVE. NEVERTHELESS, I SHOULD HAVE SHUT EVERYTHING DOWN, BUT THAT WAS A VERY DIFFICULT DECISION THAT WOULD BE BASED ON MY OPINION OF WELL KNOWN DIRECTOR BEING TOTALLY INCOMPETENT. I FENCE-STRADDLED UNTIL IT WAS TOO LATE AND HAD TO CROSS MY FINGERS AND HOPE FOR THE BEST. THE BEST DID NOT MATERIALIZE.

THE DAY TOM SARNOFF, GRANT TINKER AND I SAW THE FIRST ROUGHLY EDITED CUT OF THE FILM, WE KNEW IT WAS A DISASTER. WHEN THE LIGHTS CAME ON, GRANT TIMKER TURNED TO THE DIRECTOR, AND MORE BRUSQUELY THAN I EVER HEARD HIM, SAY, "WHAT DID YOU HAVE IN MIND WHEN YOU SHOT THIS SCRIPT, IT'S A MESS. YOU'RE FIRED. I'M TURNING WHAT WE HAVE OVER TO JOHN."

WHEN THE VERY ANGRY, OBSCENTY SPEWING DIRECTOR, BARRY SHEER, HAD LEFT, TOM SAID, "THAT WAS ONE THE BEST SCRIPTS I'D EVER READ." GRANT AND I AGREED. GRANT TURNED AND ASKED ME, "WHAT DO THINK YOU CAN DO?"

I ANSWERED HONESTLY, "I DON'T KNOW. RIGHT NOW I'M SO FRUSTRATED AND DISAPPOINTED THAT I'LL HAVE GIVE IT SOME THOUGHT AND START BY GOING THROUGH EVERY FOOT OF FILM WE HAVE AND TRY TO PUT SOMETHING TOGETHER THAT'S SHOWABLE." WE WERE ALL SO VERY ANGRY; WE'D HAD SUCH ENTHUSIASM FOR THE PROJECT.

I HAD SOME OF THE ACTORS COME IN AND DO VOICE-OVERS FOR CERTAIN SCENES. STILLS INSTEAD OF THE ORIGINAL SCENES WERE INCORPORATED. I HAD GHANGED WHAT I COULD THROUGH EDITING AND ADJUSTING. THE NEW VERSION HAD BEEN SENT TO THE SAME PROJECTION ROOM. WE HAD A SLIGHTLY LARGER AUDIENCE THIS TIME AND WHEN THE LIGHTS CAME ON, THE CONSENSUS WAS THAT WE DIDN'T HAVE TO BE EMBARASSED SENDING THIS PILOT TO NEW YORK. THE PROJECT, HOWEVER, WAS NOT VIEWED WORTHY OF A NETWORK SLOT.

SUE AND I HAD DINNER WITH DON RICKLES AND TOLD HIM OF THE DECISION. HE DIDN'T SEEM SURPRISED OR DISAPPOINTED. HE SIMPLY ACCEPTED THAT THE SHOW WOULD NOT BE GIVEN AIRTIME.HE HAD BEEN A PLEASURE TO WORK WITH FROM DAY ONE.

AT A LUNCH WITH BILL BLATTY, I TOLD HIM THAT NBC HAD DECIDED NOT TO GO AHEAD WITH PLOTKIN. ALL HE HAD TO SAY WAS, "THAT'S THE WAY THE COOKIE CRUMBLES." THE WRITER OF "SHOT IN THE DARK" HAD OTHER FISH TO FRY. NBC PRODUCTIONS SUFFERED A SETBACK WHEN OUR RECONSTRUCTED PILOT WAS NOT FAVORABLY RECEIVED IN NEW YORK. THOUGH IT WAS DIFFICULT, I HAD TO BE PUT THE SETBACK ASIDE AND PAY FULL ATTENTION TO THE OTHER TWO PROGRAMS.

"T.H.E. CAT," TURNED OUT TO BE AN OUTSTANDING PILOT. THE BEST EVER SHOT SOME PEOPLE THOUGHT AND SAID. IT WAS SHOWN AND SOLD IMMEDIATELY. WE STARTED PRODUCTION FOR TWENTY-SIX EPISODES, BORIS SEGAL TO DIRECT AND PRODUCE.

WE BEGAN PREPRODUCTION FOR, "CAPTAIN NICE." IF THE PILOT WAS APPROVED, THE SERIES COULD BE A MID-SEASON REPLACEMENT.

:

CHAPTER

22

SUE AND I FOUND OURSELVES IN A RELATIONSHIP EXCEEDING OUR HIGHEST EXPECTATIONS. WE WERE VERY MUCH LIKE A PERFECTLY MATCHED MARRIED COUPLE WITH A SHORT, BUT PLEASUREABLE HISTORY. I HAD LONG SINCE LEARNED OF WHY CHICAGO AND HER NOT WANTING GO THERE ENTERED OUR COMVERSATION DURING OUR FIRST DINNER TOGETHER. DR. MORTIMER ADLER WAS LEAVING THE SAN FRANCISCO PHILOSOPHICAL SOCIETY AND GOING BACK TO THE MIDWEST TO BE CLOSE BY THE UNIVERSITY OF CHICAGO. SUE DECLINED GOING WITH HIM, NOT WANTING TO FACE THE CRUEL WINTERS THERE. SHE GASED UP HER MARK IX JAGUAR AND DROVE DOWN TO LOS ANGELES. IF IT WASN'T FOR HER DISLIKE OF FRIGID WEATHER, WE WOULD NEVER HAVE MET.

AFTER FINDING AN APARTMENT AND MOVING IN, SUE STOPPED BY TO SAY HELLO TO HENRY GRONICH, AN OLD FRIEND AND THE OWNER OF ALPINE IMPORTERS ON LA CIENGEA BLVD. HE ASKED HER TO HELP HIM OUT FOR A FEW DAYS. SHE HAD THE TIME SO SHE GAVE HIM A COUPLE DAYS ONLY TO FIND TWO MONTHS LATER SHE WAS RUNNING THE PLACE AS MANAGER WITH A HEFTY RAISE IN PAY.

THINKING AND ACTING LIKE A MARRIED COUPLE WE HAD OUR DAILY ROUTINES. IN THE MORNING, SUE WOULD MAKE THE COFFEE AND I WOULD GO OUT FOR THE PAPER. ONE MORNING I OPENED THE DOOR TO FIND A PERSON SLEEPING. I LOOKED DOWN AND SAW THAT THE PERSON WAS MY DAUGHTER, DARRAGH. I CALLED FOR SUE. MY CALLING SUE WOKE DARRAGH. SHE YAWNED AND SAID, CALMLY, "I'M OKAY, DAD."

"WHAT IN THE WORLD ARE YOU DOING HERE, LIKE THIS," WAS ALL I COULD SAY BEFORE SUE ARRIVED.

DARRAGH GOT TO HER FEET, WITH MY HELP, AND WE WALKED INSIDE WHERE SHE EXPLAINED, "A FRIEND DROPPED ME OFF LATE LAST NIGHT. I DIDN'T WANT TO WAKE YOU UP." SHE SAT ON THE COUCH, YAWNED AGAIN, AND SAID, "I WANT TO LIVE WITH YOU, DAD, NOT AT HOME."

THE THREE OF US TALKED FOR OVER AN HOUR. SUE AND I ASSURED HER THAT WE'D LOVE TO HAVE HER WITH US, BUT ARRANGEMENTS HAD TO BE MADE, LIKE LIVING CLOSER TO HER HIGH SCHOOL. I CONVINCED HER THAT WE WOULD WORK THINGS OUT AS QUICKLY AS POSSIBLE. I DROVE HER HOME, WENT IN TO TELL RICKI THAT DARRAGH HAD BEEN WITH US FOR THE NIGHT AND HAD FORGOTTEN TO CALL. I LIED, WITH PURPOSE.

I WANTED TO BELIEVE THAT MY MEETING SUE OCCURRED BY MERGING, SEEMINGLY UNRELATABLE INCIDENTS. THE HAPPENING HAD BROUGHT CONTENTMENT AND INCREDIBLE HAPPINESS TO TWO

PEOPLE. OPENING THE FRONT DOOR OF THE APARTMENT THAT MORNING AND FINDING MY DAUGHTER CURLED UP THERE ON THE STOOP WAS SOMETHING THAT COULD HAVE BEEN TOO DISRUPTIVE FOR OUR NEWLY FOUND, ORDERLY LIVES TO TOLERATE. INSTEAD, WHAT WE DID AFTER THE "STOOP" INCIDENT MADE THE RELATIONSHIP EVEN STRONGER.

SUE AND I BOUGHT A HOUSE THAT WAS NOT TOO FAR FROM DARRAGH'S HIGH SCHOOL. WE WERE BOTH BUSY AND ASK THE OWNER OF THE FRENCH HILL, TOM DAWSON, WHO BY NOW HAD BECOME A GOOD FRIEND, TO HELP US FURNISH IT.

THOUGH MY FEELINGS FOR SUE HAD DEEPENED INTO A LOVE I HAD NEVER EXPECTED TO EXPERIENCE AGAIN, I WAS STILL WARY OF TAKING THAT FINAL STEP TO TOTAL COMMITMENT. SUE AND I DISCUSSED HOW WE BOTH FELT ABOUT OUR BECOMING A FAMILY, AND AGREED THAT WE'D FORGET THE MORES OF THE SIXTIES AND GO TO OUR TRADITIONAL ROOTS AND GET MARRIED, WITH DARRAGH IN ATTENDANCE.

WE HAD A VERY NICE, QUIET CEREMONY PERFORMED BY A JUDGE UNDER A TREE IN BEVERLY HILLS. WHEN ESCROW CLOSED ON THE HOUSE, THE THREE OF US MOVED IN WITH CLOTHES, TWO BEDS AND A COFFEE MAKER. TALENTED TOM DAWSON TURNED IT INTO A CHARMING HOME FOR THREE. RICKI DID NOT QUESTION DARRAGH'S DECISION TO LIVE WITH US, NOR DID SHE CALL ME. I BOUGHT DARRAGH A CAR TO DRIVE TO SCHOOL, NOT A VOLKSWAGON AS SHE WANTED BUT AN OLDER, HIDEOUSLY WRONG, OLD, REPAINTED CADILAC. SHE HATED IT, LOOKED SO SILLY DRIVING IT, BUT SHE WAS PROTECTED BY ITS BULK. IT WAS A CIVILIAN TANK.

TOM DAWSON WAS A WORKER OF MIRACLES. HE HAD THE FLOORS STRIPPED AND STAINED BLACK. WE BOUGHT AT HIS COST A BLACK AND WHITE FORYUNI COUCH, A PAIR OF FRENCH STYLED END TABLES, A LARGE, CUT-TO-SIZE, DEEP GREEN AREA CARPET, DEEP COMFORTABLE CHAIRS, A BEAUTIFUL FRENCH DESK AND CHAIR, A COFFEE TABLE THAT HE HAD MADE, TALL ANTIQUE CANDLE STICKS WIRED AND TOPPED BY BLACK SHADES, A MIRROR IN AN OLD GOLD LEAFED HEAVY FRAME, CHESTS FOR THE BED ROOMS, A DESK AND CHAIR FOR DARRAGH, A STUNNING, DARK SPREAD FOR OUR KING SIZED BED, A ROUND TABLE AND REFINISHED OLD WICKER CHAIRS FOR THE SMALL DINING ROOM. HE REMOVED TWO WALLS CREATING A LANAI WITH A TWO-WAY FIREPLACE AND BOOKENDED THE TWO OPENINGS WITH SHEER, YELLOW DRAPERIES. IT SEEMED AS IF OVERNIGHT WE WERE SETTLED IN OUR NEW SOMEWHAT CHIC, BUT COMFORTABLE AND INVITING HOME.

CHAPTER

23

T.H.E. CAT MADE ITS FIRST PUBLIC APPEARANCE IN SEPTEMBER, 1966 TO EXCELLENT REVIEWS. WE WERE SURE WE HAD A HIT. SIMULTANEOUS TO ITS DEBUT WE STARTED SHOOTING EPISODES OF CAPTAIN NICE WIH BUCK HENRY PRODUCING. I HAD TWO OFFICES, ONE AT PARAMOUNT STUDIOS, WHERE BOTH SHOWS WERE BEING SHOT, AND MY OFFICE IN NBC'S ADMINISTRATION BUILDING IN BURBANK. THERE, I INTERVIEWED PEOPLE IN SEARCH OF NEW PROJECTS. TWO WRITERS WERE CONTRACTED FOR SCRIPTS. NOTWITHSTANDING PLOTKIN PRISON'S FAILING, NBC PRODUCTIONS WAS LOOKING GOOD. AN AGENT, BILL COOPER, MET WITH ME TO DISCUSS PUTTING TOGETHER AN INDEPENDENT PRODUCTION COMPANY. I WAS IN THE VERY HIGHEST OF SPIRTS. MY LIFE WITH SUE AND MY NBC LIFE WERE IN WORKING AND EMOTIONAL BALANCE AND I WANTED DESPERATELY FOR THAT NEW FOUND SYNERGY TO NEVER END.

THAT IDEALISTIC BALANCE WAS SHATTERED BY THE SCOURGE OF ALL TV SHOWS, THE LACK OF AUDIENCE. NOT ENOUGH PEOPLE TUNED IN TO WATCH "T.H.E. CAT" OR "CAPTAIN NICE." BOTH WERE CANCELLED AT THE END OF THEIR RUN. I WAS TOLD THE REASON FOR THE "CAPTAIN'S" DEMISE: IT WAS SATIRE AND TV VIEWERS WERE NOT YET READY FOR THE USE OF RIDICULE OR IRONY NO MATTER HOW CLEVERLY PRESENTED.

THERE WAS ONLY ONE EXPLANATION FOR "CAT." IT AIRIED ON FRIDAY NIGHT, A NIGHT OF THE WEEK FOR GOING OUT INSTEAD OF SITTING AT HOME WATCHING TELEVISION. OUR PILOT AND THE EARLY EPISODES WERE SO OUTSTANDING THAT NEW YORK MAY HAVE THOUGHT "T.H.E. CAT" STRONG ENNOUGH TO OVERCOMING WHAT HAD BEEN TRADITIONALLY, "THE FRIDAY NIGHT KILLER OF RATINGS." THEY WERE WRONG TO CHALLENGE A CULTURAL HABIT OF "GOING OUT" AT THE END OF THE WORK WEEK. THOUGH THAT MAY BE TRUE, THE CANCELATIONS INDICATED THERE WOULD BE CHANGES AT NBC. THE FIRST OF THOSE CHANGES WAS THE SHUTTING DOWN OF NBC PRODUCTIONS. THOUGH ANTICIPATED, IT WAS HARD TO TAKE. ALL THOUGHTS FOR FORMING MY OWN PRODUCTION COMPANY VANISHED LIKE A PUFF OF SMOKE IN A HIGH WIND. I WAS, OF COURSE, DISSAPPOINTED. IN HOLLYWOOD YOU DON'T GET MANY CHANCES TO GRAB THE GOLD RING. I GOT THE BRASS ONE, AND I SERIOUSLY BEGAN TO QUESTION MY FUTURE WITH NBC.

SUE AND I DECIDED TO TAKE SOME TIME FOR OURSELVES. WE CHOSE TO VACATION IN OUR HOUSE RATHER THAN IN LAGUNA BEACH, OUR FAVORITE PLACE AWAY FROM HOLLYWOOD. AFTER A WEEK OF REHABILITATION, I WAS READY TO GO BACK AND RESUME THE DUTIES OF DIRECTOR OF FILM DEVELOPMENT. I REALLY DID NOT WANT TO DO THAT, BUT BEING FORCED TO GIVE UP A HARD EARNED CORPORATE CAREER WAS NOT TO MY LIKING EITHER.

IN 1969, GRANT TINKER LEFT NBC TO FORM MARY TYLER MOORE ENTERPRISES WITH HIS WIFE MARY. HIS REPLACEMENT WAS HERB SCHLOSSER A FORMER WALL STREET LAWYER. HERB AND I DID NOT SEE EYE TO EYE ON ANYTHING, PRIMARILY BECAUSE HE THOUGHT IN TERMS OF CONTRACTS AND I IN PROGRAMING. IT WAS NOT AND NEVER WOULD BE A GOOD WORKING RELATIONSHIP.

THE CANCELLATIONS OF "T.H.E.CAT" AND "CAPTAIN NICE," THE SHUTTING DOWN OF NBC PRODUCTIONS COMBINED WITH THE LOSS OF EXCITING NEW OPPORTUNITIES BECAME MORE AND MORE DIFFICULT TO DEAL WITH EACH PASSING DAY. DOING WHAT I HAD DONE AND HAD, TEMPOARILY, FELT THE HIGHLY CHARGED BENEFITS OF PERSONAL ACHIEVMENT WAS NOT SOMETHING I WANTED TO DO AGAIN. NOR DID I HAVE THE OLD INTEREST OR DRIVE THAT HAD ME DOING WHAT I HAD DONE BEFORE NBC PRODUCTIONS. I HAD GONE BACKWARDS, NOT AHEAD, WHICH IS AN OBOMINATION TO MOST LIBERATED HUMANS.

SUE I WERE SITTING QUIETLY ONE EVENING WHEN I SAID WITHOUT A PREAMBLE, "I DIDN'T MIND THE LONG, SOMETIMES TEDIOUS, HOURS I SPENT AT NBC PRODUCTIONS AS LONG AS THERE WAS A REWARD AT THE END. AND MY PERSONAL REWARD WAS TO MOVE FORWARD.

"NOW, HOWEVER, THAT NBC PRODUCTIONS HAS BEEN DISBANDED I'M BACK TO BEING THE HEAD OF PROGRAM DEVELOPMENT AND I'M DOING WHAT I REALLY DON'T WANT TO DO, AND THERE ARE NO REWARDS TO LOOK FOREWARD TO. THOUGH IT IS FRIGHTENING, I WANT TO LEAVE THE FAMILIAR FOR SOMETHING NEW, SOMETHING THAT'S A FAR CRY FROM RATINGS, FROM TRYING TO SATISFY AN AUDIENCE'S NEED FOR A MOMENT'S DIVERSION IN THE COURSE OF THEIR LIVES."

SUE SAID, "IT SOUNDS AS IF YOU'VE HEARD OR READ THAT NEW BEGININGS WERE THE BEST THINGS IN THE WORLD. HAVE YOU COSIDERED A NEW BEGINNING?"

I DID'NT RESPOND TO THAT DIRECTLY, BUT SAID, "A TELEVISION CAREER CAN BE LIKE A ROLLER COASTER RIDE WITH EACH SPEEDY DIP A SHOCKING LET-DOWN RATHER THAN A TURN-ON. I WONDER IF WE WOULD GET PASSED THIS DISRUPTIVE DIP IF WE COULD FIND A MORE INTERSTING WAY OF LIFE. DO WE HAVE THE COURAGE TO MAKE A CHANGE?"

THAT DISCUSSION WASN'T COMPLICATED, AND AS A VERY WISE MAN ONCE SAID, "TALK IS CHEAP." IT TOOK AN AGONIZING YEAR FOR US TO BE WISE AND GUTSY ENOUGH FOR ME TO TAKE THE FIRST STEP TOWARD A NEW BEGINNING BY RESIGNING FROM NBC.

CHAPTER

24

DARRAGH WAS AT CHOUNARD ART INSTUTE WORKING TOWARD HER DEGREE. MY SON WAS IN THE AIR FORCE AND RICKI WAS DOING EXTREMELY WELL AT VANDUESN GREEN. DUE TO THE SUCCESS OF HER BUSINESS AND MY SUDDEN LACK OF INCOME, MY OBLIGATION OF ALIMONY ENDED. I CALLED HER TO EXPLAIN AND SHE ME CUT OFF SAYING THAT THAT WAS OKAY WITH HER. RICKI EVENTUALLY SOLD THE BUSINESS TO ARLEN AND RETIRED.

WE SOLD OUR HOUSE AND PUT OUR FURNTURE IN STORAGE. SUE LEFT ALPINE IMPORTERS AND WE HEADED NORTH TO CARMEL, SAN FRANCISCO, PORTLAND AND SEATTLE HOPING TO FIND A WAY TO JUSTIFY RELOCACTING. WE RETURNED, NOT HAVING FOUND ANY THING THAT WE THOUGHT WOULD WORK FOR US AND DROVE DIRECTLY TO WHERE WE SHOULD HAVE GONE IN THE FIRST PLACE, LAGUNA BEACH. WE STAYED IN A FRIEND'S WEEKEND HOUSE AND QUICKLY DECIDED THIS IS WHERE WE WANTED TO BE. IT FELT AS THOUGH IT WAS THE RIGHT THING TO DO. AND IT TURNED OUT TO BE JUST THAT, THE RIGHT THING TO DO.

SUE AND I BEGAN A HAPPY TIME LIVING IN LAGUNA. TOGETHER WE WORKED HARD TO ESTABLISHE A HIGHLY REGARDED STOREFRONT BUSINESS ON THE COAST HIGHWAY. IT WAS A CHIC SHOP FILLED WITH GORGEOUS PLANTS, ANTIQUES, CACHEPOTS, LOCAL ART AND EVERY KIND OF BASKET WE COULD FIND. WE CALLED IT THE "PLANT PALACE." WE FOUND AND BOUGHT A VERY NICE HILLSIDE HOUSE THAT LACKED ONLY AN OCEAN VIEW. EVEN THOUGHH OUR BUSINESS WAS SELF-OPERATED WE MADE SURE THAT THERE WAS TIME TO THOROUGHLY ENJOY THE LAID-BACK LIFESTYLE OF AN EASYGOING BEACH COMMUNITY. WE JOINED THE LAGUNA NIGEL COUNTRY CLUB AND PLAYED TENNIS AFTER WORK AND ON SUNDAYS. IT DID NOT TAKE LONG FOR BOTH OF US TO SEE THAT MY LEAVING BEHIND A PREVILEDGED CAREER IN TELEVISION WAS NOT A SETBACK BUT A PROMOTION TO BEING EXUBERANTLY IN CONTROL OF OUR LIVES UNDER THE BRIGHT, CLEAR SKIES OF LAGUNA BEACH, CALIFORNIA.

THE LIFESTYLE OF LAGUNA WAS A SHIELD AGAINST BECOMING TO DEEPLY INVOLVED IN THE 70'S TURMOIL OCCUPING THE HEARTS, MINDS AND TEMPERS OF PEOPLE OVER THE GOING-ONS IN WASHINGTON DC.

IN THE SUMMER OF 1972, THERE WAS A POLITICALLY MOTIVATED BREAK-IN BY MEN OF PRESIDENT NIXON'S INNER CIRCLE AT THE DEMOCRATIC NATIONAL COMMITTTE IN WASHINGTON'S WATERGATE OFFICE COMPLEX. THE SCANDAL RESULTED IN FORTY-EIGHT, INCLUDING SOME OF NIXON'S TOP ADMINISTRATION OFFICIALS, BEING FOUND GUILTY AND JAILED. THERE WERE CALLS FOR NIXON'S

RESIGNATION. A THROUGH INVESTIGATION BY THE FBI REVEALED THAT THE PRESIDENT HAD TAPES OF HIS PRIVATE CONVERSATIONS IN THE OVAL OFFICE. THE TAPES WERE ORDERED RELEASED, BUT HE REFUSED CLAIMING EXECUTIVE PRIVILEGE. HE FIRED THE ASSIGNED SPECIAL PROSECUTOR IN OCTOBER OF 1973. THERE WAS AN UPROUR AND PEOPLE STARTED TALKING ABOUT IMPEACHMENT. IN MAY, 1974, THERE WAS A HUGE PROTEST PLANNED ALONG PENNSYLVANIA AVENUE WITH THOUSANDS OF MARCHERS. RIOT SQUADS AND THE NATIONAL GUARD WERE CALLED OUT. IT WAS FRIGHTENING THE U. S. OF A. LOOKED AS IF IT WAS A THIRD-WORLD COUNTRY. THE SUPREME COURT RULED, IN JULY OF 1974, AGAINST NIXON AND HIS WITHOLDING THE TAPES. HE RESIGNED IN AUGUST SAYING UNCONVINCINGLY, "I AM NOT A CROOK." THE NEXT DAY, AFTER A VERY STIFF SALUTE AND VERY AWKWARD WAVE GOODBYE, HE GOT INTO A HELICOPTER TO ROAR AWAY LEAVING THE COUNTRY TO RECOVER A SENSE OF WELLBEING.

WE, THE RESIDENTS OF LAGUNA BEACH EXPERIENCED IT ALL ON TELEVISION. WE WERE APPALLED AND CONCERNED, BUT NEVER GAVE UP OUR SENSE OF SUN-DRENCHED NORMALITY OR OUR LAID-BACK COMMONALITY. SUE AND I WERE GRATEFUL WHEN IT WAS OVER WITH NIXON WALKING THE BEACH IN DISGRACE BUT SAFELY IN NEARBY SAN CLEMENTE.

IN EARLY JULY OF 1978 DAVID GARRIS, A REAL ESTATE AGENT THAT WE HAD LOOKING FOR A HOUSE WE COULD BUY WITH A VIEW, CAME TO US WITH A NEW LISTING HE THOUGHT WAS JUST WHAT WE WERE LOOKING FOR, AND HE WAS RIGHT. THIS LAGUNA COTTAGE SAT ON A NARROW STRIP OF LAND ABOVE THE LAGUNA HOTEL WITH A 180 DEGREE VIEW NORTH, SOUTH AND OUT TO THE OCEAN. WE FELL IN LOVE AT FIRST SIGHT AND AFTER THE WALK THROUGH MADE AN IMMEDIATE OFFER THAT WAS LATER ACCEPTED. DAVID PUT OUR HOUSE ON THE MARKET WITH ASSURANCES THAT IT WOULD SELL QUICKLY.

ABOUT SIX WEEKS LATER, WE HAD TO FACE WHAT TURNED OUT TO BE TWO CONTRAVENING HAPPENINGS. NOT ONLY HAD WE NOT SOLD OUR HOUSE, BUT HAD ONLY A FEW LOOKERS. IT WAS CLOSE TO CLOSING AND NEITHER OF US WANTED TO CARRY TWO MORTAGES WHILE WAITING FOR A BUYER FOR OUR VIEWLESS, BUT COMFORTABLE HOME.

WE TOOK DAVID TO LUNCH AND TOLD HIM HOW DISSAPOINTED WE WERE AND EXPAINED OUR POSITION. HE, OF COURSE, COUNTERED EVERY THING WITH REAL ESTATE LOGIC. I TOLD HIM THAT WE WOULD PAY PRO RATA AMOUNTS OF THE SELLER'S TAXES, INTEREST ON THEIR MORTGAGE AND OTHER REASONABLE EXPENSES THEY'D ACCRUED FOR THE PERIOD OF TIME WE HAD THEIR PROPERTY OFF THE MARKET. WE HAD CREATED AN UNPLEASANT LUNCHEON INCIDENT THAT CIRCUMSTANCE HAD FORCED UPON US.

ON A MONDAY MORNING AT 5:55 AM, ON OCTOBER 2nd 1978, THE CITY OF LAGUNA BEACH SUFFERED A CATASTROPHY. A LANDSLIDE IN BLUE BIRD CANYON DESTROYED NINETEEN HOMES AND PARTS OF FOURTEEN OTHERS. I WAS OUT ON MY EARLY WALK, AND WHEN I RETURNED SUE MET ME AT THE DOOR TO TELL ME THAT SEVERAL PEOPLE HAD CALLED TO LET US KNOW US ABOUT THE DISASTER. I TOOK OFF MY SHORTS AND PUT ON A PAIR OF PANTS, WENT TO OUR PLANT PALACE VAN AND DROVE UP SUMMIT DRIVE TO LOOK ACROSS TO THE NORTH OF THE CANYON. I SAT FROZEN AND LIGHT HEADED. THE LAGUNA CHARMER THAT WE DIDN'T WANT BADLY ENOUGH TO CARRY TWO MORTAGES,

THE HOUSE WITH A FABULOUS VIEW THAT WE HAD WANTED TO LIVE IN FOR THE REST OF OUR LIVES WAS GONE WITH ITS SPITE OF LAND. ALL LAY BURIED AT THE BOTTOM OF THE RAVINE.

I THOUGHT SUE COULD HAVE BEEN IN THAT HOUSE ASLEEP. I WAS NOW FLOODED WITH RELIEF KNOWING SHE HAD NOT BEEN, BUT I WAS STILL PARALIZED. I GOT MY CLUTCHING RIGHT HAND OFF THE STEERING WHEEL, TURNED THE KEY IN THE IGNITION AND DROVE HOME TO TELL SUE THE GOOD AND BAD NEWS. WE SAT AT THE KITCHEN TABLE WITH CUPS OF COFFEE NOT SPEAKING. FINALLY SUE SAID, "DO YOU THINK WE DESERVE TO BE SO LUCKY?"

I SAID, "I DON'T KNOW. WHAT DO YOUT THINK YOUR FRIEND MORTIMER ADLER WOULD SAY?"

SHE JUST LOOKED AT ME, NOT ATTEMPTING TO ANSWER THAT.

I FINALLY OFFERED THIS AS SOLACE. " I BELIEVE, I STARTED SLOWLY, THAT WE MUST LIVE AND DEAL WITH WHAT EVER LIFE BRINGS US, THE FAVORABLE AND THE DISAGEEABLE, THE SATISFYING AND THE DISPLEASING, THE WONDERFUL AND THE SECOND-RATE, THE DAYS OF OUTRAGOUS LUCK AND THE DAYS OF BRAZEN BAD LUCK."

SUE REPLIED, "WELL, TODAY I'VE USED UP AN OUTRAGOUSLY GOOD LUCK DAY. I WONDER HOW MANY MORE I HAVE LEFT?"

WE DIDN'T PONDER THAT. THERE WAS'NT TIME. IT WAS A BUSINESS DAY SO WE LEFT TO OPEN OUR SHOP DOORS NOT TO SELL BUT LISTEN TO STORIES ABOUT FRIENDS WHO HAD LIVED IN AND LOVED BLUE BIRD CANYON.

 ALL DAY WE THOUGHT AND TALKED ABOUT ALL OF PEOPLE INVOLVED IN THE TRAGEDY. I HAD A FEELING OF DISENGAGEMENT, A REMOTENESS WELLED UP OFTEN AND MADE IT DIFFICULT TO BREATHE. IT WAS BIZARRE BUT I WAS FLOATING, UNATTACHED TO THE COAST HIGHWAT OR THE PLANT PALACE. IT WAS HAUNTING THAT PERCEPTION OF VULNERABLITY AND AT TIMES UNNERVING, ESPECIALLY THAT NIGHT WHEN WE LEARNED THE SLIDE HAD CONTINUED AND BY NIGHT FALL FIFTY HOMES HAD BEEN DESTROYED OR BADLY DAMAGED.

A WEEK PAST BUT I COULDN'T SHAKE THE FEELING AND KNEW THAT I COULDN'T STAY IN A HALF STUPOR AND RUN A DEMANDING BUSINESS. I FINALLY LOOKED REALISTICALLY AT WHAT HAD HAPPENED AND FOR THE FIRST TIME SAW THAT A PERSONAL DISASTER HAD BEEN AVOIDED BY MAKING AN UNPLEASANT, BUT PRACTICAL DECISION PRIOR TO THE COLLAPSE OF BLUE BIRD CANYON. ONE CAN NOT GO AROUND THINKING THEY'RE FOREVER SAFE IN THIS DIVERSE WORLD. I'M SURE MARTIN LUTHER KING, BECAUSE OF HIS GOOD WORKS, FELT FREE FROM DANGER, BUT WAS STILL GUNNED DOWN ON AN OPEN BALCONY SURROUNDED BY SUPORTERS. REALITY BROUGHT ME BACK TO HOW THINGS ARE IN THIS WORLD WE INHABIT.

CHAPTER

25

OUR VILLAGE BY THE SEA WAS NO LONGER EASYGOING. IT SEEMED AS THOUGH EVERYBODY WANTED TO LIVE IN LAGUNA BEACH. IT HAD BECOME A THRIVING CITY WITH TRAFFIC JAMS ON THE WEEKENDS. REAL ESTATE VALUES SKYROCKETED AND PROPERTIES SOLD QUICKLY TO INVESTORS. OUR HOME, THE ONE THAT DIDN'T SELL, ROSE IN VALUE TO BE WORTH FIVE TIMES WHAT WE PAID FOR IT. WE DECIDED TO TAKE CONTROL OF THE OUT-OF-HAND SITUATION BY SELLING THE BUSINESS, OUR HOME AND BECOME RETIREES IN PRESCOTT, A DELIGHTFUL, MILE-HIGH CITY IN NORTHERN ARIZONA.

A DECISION, BORN OF AN OPPORTUNITY TO SELL BOTH THE BUSINESS AND OUR RESIDENCE AT EXAGGERATED PRICES, BROUGHT US TO PRESCOTT, A CITY HIGH ABOVE THE DESERT LANDS OF ARIZONA. IT BOASTED ITS FOUR WELL DEFINED, BUT MILD SEASONS, ITS CENTRALIZED COURTHOUSE AND THE COMMUNITY SPIRIT IT PROMOTED AND SUPPORTED. I WAS SOON ON THE BOARD OF DIRECTORS FOR THE LOCAL ADULT CENTER. ONCE AGAIN I BECAME A CONTRIBUTOR TO A COMMUNITY. I WAS ELECTED PRESIDENT OF THE BOARD AND THAT WAS INTERESTING AND FULFILLING FOR A WHILE UNTIL SEEMINGLY IN THE WINK OF AN EYE, I WAS EIGHTY YEARS OLD WITH STILL TOO MANY FREE HOURS ON MY HANDS. I RESISTED THE TRADITIONAL NOTIONS OF RETIREMENT. IT WAS UNTHINKABLE TO ALLOW NAPS, LAP ROBES AND WARM MILK TO TAKE OVER MY LIFE.

AS I TOUGHT MORE ABOUT LIVING WITH EMPTY HOURS, I REALIZED THAT MORE THAN ANYTHING ELSE I'D BEEN BORED, I WAS NOT USED TO DAYS OF INACTIVITY. I HAD TO BECOME INTERESTED IN SOMETHING THAT WAS NOI FACTUAL, FEASIBLE OR FUNCTIONAL. IT HAD TO BE COMPELLING, SOMETHING THAT REQUIRED INTELLECTUAL EXPLORATION AND EMOTIONAL COMMITMENT.

I TALKED THIS OVER WITH SUE, SEEKING HER ADVICE ON HOW I COULD FIND AN UNDERTAKING WORTHY OF TOTAL ENGAGEMENT. ONE THAT WOULD FILL THOSE WASTED HOURS. SHE SAID, "YOU HAVE HAD A PREOCCUPATION WITH CONTEMPORY ART FOR AS LONG AS I'VE KNOWN YOU. WHY NOT FOCUS ON THAT?"

SUE WAS RIGHT. CONTEMPORARY ART HAD FASCINATED AND HAD GIVEN ME PLEASURE FOR SIXTY YEARS. I STILL REMEMBER THE FIRST TIME I'D SEEN VAN GOGH'S, "THE STARY NIGHT," MATISSE'S, "THE DANCE," AND MONDRIAN'S STARTLING, "BROADWAY BOGGIE WOOGIE" ON MY MANY VISITS TO THE MUSEUMS FEATURING MODERN ART. MY VISITS TO GALLERIES HAD BEEN REWARDING AND BUYING FEW PIECES OF ORIGINAL ART IN LAGUNA AND CARMEL GRACED THE WALLS OF OUR HOME FOR CONSTANT APPRECIATION.

I HAD ALWAYS ADMIRED MOST THE PIONEERING, CONTEMPORARY ARTISTS WHO WERE THE FIRST TO BREAK FREE OF THE RESTRAINTS INVETERATE TO TRADITIONAL ART. WHILE ADMIRING THEIR INTENSE, MULTICOLORED, EXTRAVAGANT LANDSCAPES AND FIGURATIVE PAINTINGS, I HAD OFTEN HAD AN ODD

URGING TO GRASP THE FREEDOM THEY HAD PROVIDED FOR SELF-EXPRESSION. I WONDERED WHAT IT WOULD BE LIKE HAVING WHATEVER IT WAS THAT ALLOWED THEM TO BRING ABOUT A MEANS OF ACCOMPLISHING SOMETHING SO ORIGINAL, SO INDIVIDUALISTIC. I INTENDED TO FIND OUT.

SUE'SCOMMENT BECAME AN EVENT. THE NEXT MORNING, I DROVE TO THE NEAREST ART SUPPLY STORE WHERE AN EXTREMELY COMPETENT YOUNG WOMEN CHARMED ME INTO AQUIRING ALL THAT AN UNSCHOOLED, NEOPHYTE ARTIST WOULD NEED TO BECOME WORLD FAMOUS.

AT HOME, FULLY EQUIPPED, A LITTLE UNCERTAINTY SET IN. HOW DOES ONE AT EIGHTY AND UNSCHOOLED START A PAINTING?

SEEKING SOME KIND OF GUIDANCE, I WENT TO THE BOOK SHELVES AND FOUND, "THE ARTS OF MAN." LEAFING THROUGH IT, I CAME TO MATISSE'S, "THE PURPLE ROBE." HIS BOLD, BLACK OUTLINING OF A WOMAN SEATED IN BACK OF LOW TABLE WITH FLOWERS LOOKED LIKE SOMETHING I COULD DO. AFTER ALL, DIDN'T I DRAW FAIRLY WELL WHEN A KID?

DID I FEAR BEING HEAVILY INFLUENCED BY THE WORK OF SOMEONE ELSE? NOT AT ALL. EVERYTHING THAT COULD BE DONE WITH CANVAS, BRUSH AND PAINT HAD BEEN DONE. ANYTHING I WOULD DO WOULD BE REFLECTIVE, BUT IT HAD TO BE WHAT I LIKED.

I UNWRAPPED A SMALL CANVAS, OPENED A BOTTLE OF BLACK ACRYLIC PAINT, DIPPED IN ONE OF MY BRUSHES AND OUTLINED A MISSHAPEN TABLETOP AND ON IT A DEFORMED APPLE, A PEAR, A MISSHAPEN BOWL AND WINE BOTTLE. I LEFT IT ON MY DESK TO LET THE THICK PAINT DRY. I RETURNED AND FILLED IN THE VARIOUS SPACES WITH A SELECTION OF ARBITRAILY CHOOSEN, BRIGHT COLORS. THOUGH IMPATIENT TO ASSESS MY FIRST EVER PAINTING, I LEFT THE ROOM AGAIN TO LET IT DRY.

LATER, I PROPPED IT UP, STUDIED IT AND THOUGHT THAT MY CHOICE OF COLORS AND SPACES SEEM TO COME TOGETHER IN AN INTERESTING WAY. CONCERNED ABOUT MY ABILITY TO BE OBJECTIVE, I CARRIED IT IN TO SHOW SUE. SHE LOOKED AND SAID, "I LIKE IT, CAN'T TELLYOU WHY THOUGH." THERE WAS A PAUSE BEFORE, "I KNOW THAT IT'S EYE-CATCHING. LET'S LIVE WITH IT FOR A COUPLE OF DAYS."

WE BOTH STILL LIKED IT THE NEXT DAY. ENCOURAGED, I BEGAN PAINTING EVERY MORNING. I HAD NO RULES TO FOLLOW SO I ENJOYED INVENTING LANDSCAPES, STILL LIFES AND PEOPLE. COMPLETED CANVASES GREW IN NUMBER. SOME, I THOUGHT, WERE PRETTY GOOD, BUT I WONDERED IF I WAS OPEN-MINDED ENOUGH TO JUDGE. ANXIOUS TO FIND OUT, I CALLED A FRIEND, WITH A STRONG ACADEMIC BACKGROUND IN ART AND ASKED HIM TO COME OVER FOR A DRINK AND SEE WHAT I'D BEEN DOING TO AMUSE MYSELF. WE EACH HAD A SCOTCH ON THE ROCKS BEFORE I ESCORTED HIM TO MY WORK AREA. INSIDE I HAD OVER A DOZEN CANVASES SCATTERED ABOUT. HE SAID, "I DIDN'T KNOW YOU PAINTED."

"I STARTED A COUPLE OF MONTHS AGO," I TOLD HIM.

HE WANDERED AROUND, PICKED UP A FEW AND SAID, "JOHN, SOME OF THESE ARE VERY GOOD, NOT ALL."

I NODDED.

HE WENT ON SAYING, "WHEN VIEWING GOOD ART, THE VIEWER MUST SENSE THAT THE ARTIST WAS IN COMPLETE CONTROL OF HIS OR HER MEDIUM. YOU EXHIBIT THE INNOCENT FREEDOM OF AN UNSCHOOLED SELF-EXPRESSIONIST AND I LOVE THAT, BUT THERE MUST ALWAYS BE A CONSCIOUS UNIFICATION OF THE VARIOUS PARTS OF WHAT YOU'RE DEPICTING BY WAY OF CONTROL. I THINK YOU ACHIEVE THAT IN SOME OF THESE INTUITEVLY, BUT YOU'RE NOT IN COMMAND IN OTHERS. DO YOU UNDERSTAND WHAT I'M SAYING?"

"I KNEW SOME WERE BAD BUT I DIDN'T KNOW WHY. I'LL HAVE TO THINK ABOUT WHAT YOU'VE SAID."

DUI CONTINUED WITH, "IT'S IMPORTANT." HE SELECTED SIX AND PUT THEM ON MY DESK AND SAID, "I'D FRAME THESE AND TAKE THEM INTO ONE OF OUR LOCAL GALLERIES. SEE WHAT THEY HAVE TO SAY."

HE LEFT WISHING ME LUCK WTH THE SIX HE HAD PICKED OUT.

CHAPTER

26

PRESCOTT WAS, AND IS, A CITY WITH A SURPRISING NUMBER OF GALLERIES. A COUPLE OF WEEKS LATER, I BROUGHT THE SIX I'D HAD FRAMED TO "THE LOFT," ON GURLEY STREET. I INTRODUCED MYSELF AND SHOWED THE MANAGER THE SIX. HE THOUGHT THEY WOULD SELL AND WANTED ALL OF THEM. I SIGNED A SIMPLE AGREEMENT AND WENT HOME TO TELL SUE THE DUMBFOUNDING NEWS of A GALLERY WANTING THEM, AND HAVE A FEW CELEBRATORY GLASSES OF WINE

THAT IS HOW, AT THE AGE OF EIGHTY IN 2001, I STARTED TO PAINT AND FOR SIX YEARS, I WAS HAPPY PAINTING REPRESENTATIONALLY. IN 2008, MY LANDSCAPES, PORTRAITS AND STILL LIFES HAD SOLD IN FOURTEEN SHOWINGS. THEY WERE PART OF PERMANENT INVENTORIES IN FIVE GALLERIES, IN ONE I HAD A ONE MAN SHOW, AS ANNOUNCED BELOW, AND IN SEVEN OTHERS I WAS IN GROUP SHOWINGS.

MY ASSUMING THAT I DIDN'T HAVE THE RESOURSEFULNESS ACQUIRED BY YEARS OF ART EDUCATION TO MAKE USE OF THE UNBOUNDED SCOPE OF ART LIMITED ME TO PRECONCEIVING EVERYTHING I DID. TO PAINT A STILL LIFE, I PUT TOGETHER SELECTED OBJECTS IN MY HEAD AND THEN TRANSFERED THAT INTELLECTUAL VISION TO AN EMPTY CANVAS. I HAD BARRED MYSELF FROM FINDING SPONTANIOUSLY A BALANCE BETWEEN THE STRAIGHTEST LINE AND THE MOST GRACEFUL CURVE. I HAD DONE THAT BEFORE PLACING THE DUPLICATING IMAGE ON CANVAS. THEN AND NOW, I SEE THAT PROCESS TOO SIMILAR TO PUTTING A JIGSAW PUZZLE TOGETHER TO LOOK LIKE THE PICTURE ON THE BOX. HOW CREATIVE IS THAT? I DIDN'T WANT TO BE REDUCED TO WHAT WAS CAREFULLY PREPLANNED. I WANTED TO ENJOY A MORE PERSONAL PROCESS OF DISCOVERY AND TRIUMPH.

I WONDERED, THEN AND NOW, WHAT APPROACH TO MAKING ART WAS INDEPENDENT OF THE RULES I'D ACQUIRED PAINTING REPRESENTATIONLY? WHAT CAN I DO THAT DOESN'T REQUIRE THE PROPER USE OF PERSPECTIVE, OR THE PROPER USE OF PROPORTION, OR THE PROPER SELECTION OF THE MOST APPROPRIATE COLORS?

THE ANSWER, I SUDDENLY REALIZED, WAS SIMPLE, PAINT AN ABSTRACT.

IN 2008, I STARTED MY FIRST UNPLANNED PAINTING.WITH A SWEEPING STROKE OF A LUSCIOUS PURPLE. I REACHED DOWN TO THE DEEPEST LEVELS OF INTUITION AND INSTINCT AND LET IMPULSES AND GUT REACTIONS TAKE CONTROL.

FOR ALMOST SIX HOURS TRIAL AND ERROR DIRECTED PROGESSION FROM THAT ARBITRARY SLASH OF COLOR. A FRESH, UNTAPPED SIXTH SENSE TURNED THE IRREGULARITIES OF THE BRIGHTIST COLORS, ODDBALL SHAPES, AND THE DISPARITY OF LIGHT AND DARK INTO A MANY LAYERED CANVAS THAT PLEASED ME ENORMOUSLY.

BEFORE DECLARING IT A SUCCESSFUL ABSTRACT, HOWEVER, AN INTERNAL BALANCE OF ALL ITS DIVERSE PARTS HAD TO BE PRESENT AS DUI HAD SAID. I LOOKED AND SAW THAT WHAT WAS ESSENTIAL TO ALL ART WAS THERE. I HAD ACHIEVED A BALANCE OF THE DIVERSE PARTS EITHER BY LUCK OR BY ACCIDENT. CERTAINLY NOT INTELLECTUALLY WHILE I WAS IMPROVISING LIKE ACTORS AND ACTRESSES WHO CREATE ENGAGING SCENES WITHOUT A SCRIPT. EXPERIENCING SUCH ABSOLUTE FREEDOM, BEING SUSPENDED FROM DAY AND TIME WAS OVERWHELMING.

I REMEMBER IT CLEARLY BECAUSE IT WAS THE BEGINNING OF A CHANGE IN MY COURSE TO ART.

I PAINTED SEVEN MORE, NONE IN SIX HOURS. MOST REQUIRED ADJUSTMENTS THAT LASTED FOR WEEKS, AND ONE A MONTH. THE INTELLECT WAS NOT TO BE MADE LIGHT OF IT WAS FREQUENTLY CALLED UPON TO INSURE THE PRESENCE OF SYMMETRY IN EACH OF THE SEVEN. THE DAY CAME TO PUT THEM, IN MY HANDY CARRYALL, AND DRIVE A FAMILIAR ROUTE TO A GALLERY THAT HAD BEEN SHOWING MY REPRESENTATIONAL WORK. FOR THREE YEARS. UPON ARRIVAL AND AFTER ENJOYING OUR USUAL PLEASANTRIES, I LINED UP THE ABSTRACTS ON THE FLOOR AND AGAINST A WALL FOR VIEWING.

I GOT A SHOCKING RESPONSE FROM ROSEMARIE, THE OWNER. SHE SAID THAT SHE LOVED MY ABSTRACTS, BUT DIDN'T WANT THEM BECAUSE THEY WERE IMPOSSIBLE TO SELL. I KNEW SHE HAD AN ECLECTIC VIEW OF ART AS WELL AS A PRACTICAL VIEW ACQUIRED BY EXPERIENCE, SO I HAD TO ACCEPT WHAT SHE'D SAID, THOUGH IT WAS DEVASTATING, I DESPERATELY WANTED ANOTHER OPINION SO I DROVE TO A SECOND GALLERY ABOUT AN HOUR AWAY.

THERE, I GOT THE SAME RESPONSE, BUT THIS TIME, "ABSTRACTS ARE IMPOSSIBLE TO SELL IN *ARISONA*," WAS ADDED. TWO HORENDOUS JOLTS IN ONE DAY WAS TOO MUCH. VERY DISCOURAGED, I DROVE HOME WITH MY EIGHT REJECTED ABSTRACTS WAITING TO REMIND ME OF A TRULY AWFUL DAY.

IT WAS PAINFUL LIVING WITH THE REALIZATION THAT IN ORDER TO REMAIN AN ARTIST IN ARIZONA I HAD TO GIVE UP THE FREEDOM I HAD ENJOYED CREATING WITHOUT A DICTATORIAL PLAN. WHERE DID THAT LEAVE ME AND MY EIGHT UNWANTED WORKS THAT REPRESENTED A BREAKTHROUGH TO A NEW AND EXCITING WAY OF DOING WHAT I MOST WANTED TO DO?

DEPRESSED AND WALLOWING IN SELF-PITY, I SAT A FEW NIGHTS LATER STARING AT MY REBUFFED CANVASES. I WONDERED, WHY IS THE APPRECIATION OF ART SO SELCTIVE WHEN THE ELEMENTS OF ART ARE THE SAME IN ALL ART. WHY SHOULD A PLEASING ARRANGEMENT OF COLORS IN ONE BE PREFERRED AND IN ANOTHER ILLFAVORED?. WHY MUST SOMETHING FAMILIAR, SOMETHING RECOGNIZABLE BE PRESENT BEFORE SOME PEOPLE CAN APPRECIATE BEAUTY?

IF THEY MUST HAVE SOMETHING RECOGNIZABLE, I THOUGHT, WOULD A MOON IN THAT DARKISH ONE BE ENOUGH FOR THEM TO SEE WHAT I JUST SAW, AN UNUSUAL SKY? I REMEMBER I WAS AT FIRST STUNNED BY WHAT I'D ASKED MYSELF, BUT THEN I THOUGHT I'VE HAD A RARE SERENDIPITOUS MOMENT. I PICKED UP THE CANVAS AND ALMOST RAN TO MY WORK SPACE. IN NO MORE THAN A COUPLE OF MINUTES I HAD A PALE MOON RIDING A SWIRLING NIGHT SKY.

IT WAS AS IF THERE HAD BEEN A MAGIC WAND IN MY HAND INSTEAD OF A BRUSH AND IT HAD CHANGED WHAT WAS OBSCURE INTO A SKY THE LIKE OF WHICH I'D NEVER SEEN. WHETHER I HAD SEEN ONE, LIKE IT OR NOT, IT WAS NOW A SLICE OF REALITY BECAUSE SKIES CAN BE AS LIMITLESS AS CREATIVITY.

THANKFUL THAT ACRYLIC PAINT DRIES FAST, I WAITED A FEW MORE MINUTES AND TOOK THE CANVAS OUT TO SUE. SHE LOOKED STARTLED, BUT THEN SMILED BRFORE SAYING, "YOUR ABSTRACT HAS NOT ENTIRELY DISAPPEARED EVEN THOUGH IT'S BECOME AN AMAZING SKY." THERE WAS A PAUSE BEFORE, "YOU COULD CALL IT A SKYSCAPE." I AGREED, FOR IT WAS, INDEED, A SKYSCAPE.

I TURNED THE REMAINING UNWANTED NONOBJECTIVES INTO SKIES BY CONSCIOUSLY CHOOSING FOR EACH SOMETHING SUBSTANIVE AND SUITABLE, LIKE A SUN, A MOON, A BODY OF WATER OR A MOUNTAIN RANGE.

ANXIOUS FOR AN OPINION AS TO THEIR ACCEPTABILITY, I CALLED ROSEMARIE SHEMAITS, THE OWNER OF THE SPIRIT GALLERY WHERE I HAD FIRST TAKEN MY ABSTRACTS. I TOLD HER I HAD SOMETHING TO SHOW HER AND WANTED HER OPINION ON A NEW APPROACH. HER GALLERY WAS MY FAVORITE AND SHE WAS MY NUMBER ONE OWNER. SHE ASKED, "WHEN WILL I SEE YOU?"

I SAID, "TODAY IF IT'S CONVENIENT."

"COME AHEAD," WAS HER RESPONSE.. "I HAVEN'T HAD ANYONE IN ALL MORNING"

I AGAIN DROVE UP 89A TO THE HISTORIC COPPER MINING TOWN OF JEROME THAT WAS NOW A THRIVING TOURIST AND ARTIST COMMUNITY WITH A POPULATION OF ABOUT 450. WHILE ON VACATION, ROSEMARIE VISITED JEROME, LOVED EVERTHING ABOUT IT, WENT BACK TO CHICAGO, QUIT HER GRAPHIC ARTS DIRECTORSHIP IN AN ADVERTISING AGENCY, RETURNED, AND LIVED OUT A DREAM BY ESTABLISHING HER OWN GALLERY.

I ARRIVED A LITTLE AFTER TWO O'CLOCK TO FIND HER SITTING ALONE ON ONE OF HER VIEWING BENCHES. SHE GOT UP WHEN I WALKED IN AND WE GREETED EACH OTHER AS IF WE WERE THE OLDEST OF FRIENDS, BUT I SENSED SOMETHING WAS NOT RIGHT WITH HER.

"WELL, LET'S SEE WHAT YOU BROUGHT ME," SHE SAID, POINTING AT THE CANVAS BAG.

I BEGAN MY USUAL ROUTINE OF LINING UP THE CANVASES AGAINST THE WALL ACROSS FROM THE BENCH. SHE DIDN'T SIT, SHE REMAINED STANDING AND WHEN I PUT THE LAST ONE DOWN SHE SAID, "I SEE WHAT YOU'VE DONE AND IT'S BRILLIANT. YOU HAVE GIVEN A VIEWER AN OPPORTUNITY TO SEE AND APPRECIATE SOMETHING INCOMPREHENSABLE AND PERPLEXING BY TURNING THAT SOMETHING INTO AN EASILY IDENTIFIABL SKY."

"I CALL THEM SKYSCAPES," I SAID QUIETLY NOT WANTING TO BREAK HER TRAIN OF THOUGHT. I WANTED TO HEAR MORE FROM HER QUICK ANALYSIS. SHE DIDN'T DISSAPPOINT.

"EVERY WORTHY ARTIST SEEKS A SIGNITURE ART AND YOU, JOHN, HAVE FOUND YOURS. THESE SKYSCAPES ARE WHAT YOU WERE MEANT TO DO. THEY ARE UNIQUE, BOLD AND YET FRIENDLY. THAT IS VERY CLOSE TO HER EXACT WORDS.

SHE REMAINED STANDING, SMILING AND THEN SHE LOST THE SMILE SAYING, "THIS ECONOMIC DOWNTURN HAS UNEMPLOYMENT AT A HIGH OF 10%. TOO MANY PEOPLE HAVE STOPPED BUYING THINGS THEY DON'T ACTUALLY NEED - LIKE A PAINTING THAT CATCHES THEIR EYE. IT WAS TIME FOR A PERSONAL EVALUATION OF THE CIRCUSTANCES. THIS WEEK I HAD TO DECIDE WHETHER TO KEEP THE GALLERY OPEN OR CLOSE IT.

I SAID, "I KNOW SOME OF THE SMALLER GALLERIES NOT IN TOPNOTCH LOCATIONS ARE ALREADY GONE. EVEN SMALL BUSINESSES IN PRESCOTT'S GATEWAY MALL ARE FOLDING. THE MALL'S GIANT PARKING LOTS ARE ALMOST EMPTY ON A WEEKDAY. BUT I THOUGHT YOU WERE OKAY."

SHE SAID, WITH TOUCH OF ANGER SEEPING IN, "I'VE BEEN FORCED TO MAKE A DECISION. MY GOOD LOCATION HERE IN JEROME WITH ITS MANY TOURISTS HASN'T PROTECTED ME. I'LL CLOSE THE GALLERY RIGHT AFTER THE NEXT ART WALK ON NOVEMBER 7TH. SHE LOST THE ANGER LOOKING AGAIN AT THE SKYSCAPES AND SAID, "I'M GOING TO ASK YOU TO DO ME A FAVOR."

HER CLOSING THE GALLERY HIT ME HARD. A FULL IMPACT OF THE RECESSION KEPT ME TEMPORARILY MUTE EXCEPT FOR SAYING, "ANYTHING I CAN DO, I WILL, ROSEMARIE?"

"I WANT TO GO OUT WITH A BANG ON MY LAST ART WALK, LET ME HANG THOSE." SHE POINTED AT THE SKYSCAPES. "BANG" WAS THE WORD SHE USED.

I SAID, "OF COURSE YOU CAN HAVE THEM. IS THERE ANYTHING ELSE I CAN DO?"

"THERE'S NOTHING TO DO. YOU AND I CAN'T DO WHAT'S NECESSARY, BRINGING AN ABRUPT HALT TO THIS DOWNWARD SPIRAL." SHE HESITATED AND THEN SAID, "BUT THANKS FOR OFFERING."

SHE FINALLY SAT AND SO DID I. SHE CALMLY BEGAN TO OUTLINE HER SCHEDULE FOR CLOSING. TELLING ME AS IF IT WAS IMPORTANT FOR ME TO KNOW, "ON MONDAY THE 9TH, I'LL CALL OR E-MAIL ALL OF THE ARTISTS TO TELL THEM I'LL BE CLOSING FOR GOOD ON THE 1ST OF DECEMBER. AND THAT THEIR REMAINING BITS AND PIECES WILL BE READY TO PICKUP ON THE FOLLOWING WEEKEND. WHEN ALL OF

THE ART IS GONE, I'LL PATCH AND PAINT THE WALLS AND GIVE THE PLACE A THROUGH CLEANING." I REMEMBER THAT SHE ADDED, "I WANT TO GET MY DEPOSIT MONEY BACK."

FOR SOMETHING TO SAY, I SUGGESTED, "WHY DON'T I COME IN ON THE MONDAY, AFTER THE ART WALK AND GET MY THINGS OUT OF YOUR WAY?"

SHE ANSWERED ABSENTLY, "THAT WOULD BE GOOD."

SADLY, I LEFT HER WITH MY EMPTY CARRYALL IN HAND.

CHAPTER

27

ON THE DRIVE HOME, I REALIZED THAT I HAD BEEN SO PREOCCUPIED THAT I HADN'T GIVEN THE FINANCIAL CRISES THE ATTENTION IT DESERVED. A BLAMELESS FRIEND, ROSEMARIE, WAS CRUSHED BY IT BECAUSE SHE WAS GUILTY OF BEING DEEPLY COMMITTED TO A WAY OF LIFE THAT ONLY DREAMS AND A LOT OF COURAGE COULD MAKE REAL. WHAT WOULD SHE DO NOW? AND WHAT WOULD THE HUNDREDS OF OTHER ROSEMARIES DO? WHAT WOULD I DO IF MORE GALLERIES LIKE HER'S FOLDED?

I WAS SUFFICENTLY DEPRESSED TO DRIVE CAREFULLY DOWN MINGUS MOUNTAIN'S TWO LANE, SLIGHTLY DANGEROUS ROAD.

TO STAY BUSY, I PAINTED ANOTHER SKYSCAPE WITH A SLASH OF ARBITRARY COLOR AND LET INSTINCT BRING COOPERATIVE HUES AND SHAPES TOGETHER INTO A RESEMBLANCE OF BALANCE. WHEN THAT HAPPENED, I SET THE CANVAS ASIDE. LATER I LET INTUITION REFINE AND ENHANCE, TO MY SATISFACTION, WHAT I HAD. I ADDED A REAL WORLD DETAIL TO ORIENT A VIEWER. I WAS PLEASED WITH MY FIRST DELIBERATE AND INTENTIONAL SKYSCAPE. EVERY SKYSCAPE FROM THEN ON WILL BE THE RESULT NOT OF A PRECONCEPTION BUT OF PERSONAL INSIGHTS.

WHILE HOPING FOR SOMETHING TO HAPPEN SO I WOULDN'T HAVE TO MAKE MY DISTRESSING TRIP UP THE MOUNTAIN ON NOVEMBER THE 9TH. THE DAY, HOWEVER, ARRIVED AS I KNEW IT WOULD.

HER ENTRY HAD A CLOSED SIGN, BUT THE DOOR WAS OPEN. I WENT IN TO FIND ROSEMARIE DOING SOMETHIG IN THE FAR END. SHE CALLED OUT GOOD MORNING, JOHN. YOUR THINGS ARE STACKED AGAINST THE RIGHT WALL. I LOOKED OVER TO SEE WHAT WAS LEFT OF MY EARLIER WORK AND SAW ONLY ONE SKYSCAPE SET OFF TO THE SIDE.

I SAID, "I'LL TAKE THESE OUT TO THE CAR. WHERE ARE THE REST OF THE SKYSCAPES?"

SHE HAD COME UP BESIDE ME AND SAID WITH A HINT OF A SMILE, "KNOWING YOU DIDN'T BECOME AN ARTIST BECAUSE YOU NEEDED ADDITIONAL INCOME, I MADE SEVEN PEOPLE HAPPY BY PRICING YOUR SKYSCAPES FAR BELOW WHAT THEY'RE WORTH. I MADE MYSELF HAPPY BY SEEING THEM LEAVE WITH AN UNEXPECTED TREASURE. BESIDES MAKING A LIVING, ONE OF THE REWARDS OF OWNING A GALLERY WAS SEEING SOMEONE LEAVE WITH A PIECE OF OUTSTANDING ART THAT THEY NEVER THOUGHT THEY'D BE LUCKY ENOUGH TO HAVE TO LOOK AT EVERY DAY."

SURPRISED, STUNNED AND PLEASED, A COMBINATION OF EMOTIONS THAT HAD ME STANDING OPEN-MOUTHED STARING AT ROSEMARIE. WHEN I COULD SPEAK I SAID, "I'D LIKE TO BE ADDED TO YOUR LIST

OF HAPPY PEOPLE. I DREADED COMING HERE TODAY TO SEE A GREAT GALLERY ABOUT TO BE TORN APART. DO YOU HAVE TIME FOR US TO SAY GOODBYE AND GOOD LUCK OVER A CUP OF COFFEE?"

SHE WENT TO HER DESK, PICKED UP HER KEYS AND SAID, "I CAN BEGIN CONTACTING THE OTHER ARTISTS THIS AFTERNOON. LET'S GO DOWN TO JAKE'S CAFÉ AND HAVE A FRESH CROISSANT WITH THE COFFEE." (WE DID GO TO A SMALL CAFÉ, HAD CROISSANTS, BUT I'M NOT SURE IT WAS CALLED "JAKE"S." I DID THINK, "CROISSANTS IN JEROME?")

WE WALKED INTO "JAKE'S." HE LOOKED UP AND CALLED OUT, "MORNING ROSY." HE NODDED TO ME AS WE SAID GOOD MORNING IN RETURN. ROSEMARIE SAID AS WE SAT AT A LITTLE TABLE, "TWO COFFEES AND TWO CROISSANTS, JAKE."

THE PASTRIES WERE DELIICIOUS. WE DEVOURED THEM WHILE EXCHANGING VIEWS ON THE MISFORTUNES BROUGHT ON BY THE RUINOUS RECESSION. WE HAD COFFEE REFILS AND THEN I ASK ROSEMARIE WHAT SHE WAS GOING TO DO AFTER THE CLOSING OF HER GALLERY.

SHE SAID SHE WASN'T SURE, BUT WOULD TAKE HER TIME AND HOPEFULLY MAKE THE RIGHT DECISION. SHE ADDED THAT SHE HAD SOME RESERVE MONEY THAT SHE HADN'T WANTED TO RISK BY KEEPING THE GALLERY OPEN. SHE FOLLOWED THAT WITH, "THIS FINANCIAL SITUATION WILL RIGHT ITSELF, BUT UNFORTUNATELY NOBODY KNOWS HOW LONG IT WILL TAKE. WHAT EVERBODY IN ART KNOWS IS THAT IF IT CONTINUES ONLY THE HIGH-END GALLERIES REPRESENTING THE MOST WELL KNOWN ARTISTS WILL SURVIVE."

I SAT QUIETLY FOR A MOMENT MULLING THAT OVER. AND THEN ROSESEMARIE ASKED, "WHAT WILL YOU DO WHEN ALL THE GALLERIES THAT BRING ART TO MIDDLE AMERICA ARE GONE?"

I ANSWERED, "I DON'T KNOW. I DO KNOW THAT I'LL MISS HAVING MY SELF-TAUGHT THINGS ON DISPLAY. THERE'S A SPECIAL PLEASURE IN BEING SELF-TAUGHT AND DOING SOMETHING WELL ENOUGH TO BE ACKNOWLEDGED BY PEOPLE WHO HAVE A HIGH STAKE IN THE SELLING OF ART. THERE IS SOMETHING EVEN MORE SPECIAL: HAVING SOMEONE LIKE YOUR WORK WELL ENOUGH TO BUY IT."

SHE NODDED HER UNDERTANDING. AFTER ANOTHER SIP OF HER SECOND REFILL OF COFFEE, SHE SAID, "I KNOW WHAT I'D LIKE TO DO."

INTERESTED, I SAID, "WHAT'S THAT?"

"I WOULD LIKE TO WORK IN ONE THOSE HIGH-END GALLERIES." WITH A WEAK SMILE SHE ADDED, "THE TYPE OF GALLERY THAT IS CAPABLE OF WITHSTANDING FLOODS, EARTHQUAKES AND, OF COURSE, RECESSIONS. I MAY DRIVE TO SAN FRANCISCO AND OFFER MY SERVICES TO ONE THAT'S STILL GOING STRONG. I DON'T WANT TO GO BACK TO ANOTHER CHICAGO WINTER."

"I DON'T BLAME YOU. I'VE BEEN THERE AND DONE THAT."

"WOULD YOU MIND MY TELLING YOU WHAT I WOULD DO IF I WAS YOU?"

ALL I SAID WAS, "PLEASE DO."

"YOU DON'T HAVE A COMPUTER DO YOU?"

"I'VE NEVER WANTED ONE OR THOUGHT THAT I NEEDED ONE."

"WELL, YOU'RE GOING TO NEED A COMPUTER NOW SO I'D GO TO WALMART AND BUY ONE. THEN, I WOULD HIRE AN AT-HOME TUTOR WHO'S CAPABLE OF TEACHING ME HOW TO PUT TOGETHER AN ELECTRONIC PORTFOLIO WITH PICURES OF YOUR SKYSCAPES AND A BRIEF BIO. I'D STAY BUSY WHILE WAITING FOR THE RECESSION TO BOTTOM OUT BY PAINTING MORE SkYSCAPES. WHEN THE ECONOMY IS HEALTHIER, I'D GO TO MY COMPUTER AND FIND A GALLERY SHOWING ART THAT MY SKYSCAPES WOULD BE COMPATIBLE HANGING NEXT TO. I'D WASTE NO TIME SENDING MY ELECTRONIC PORTFOLIO TO THAT GALLERY." THERE WAS A PAUSE BEFORE SAYING, "CONTACTING GALLERIES AROUND THE WORLD IS NOW AS SIMPLE AS PRESSING A LIGHT SWITCH. THE DAYS OF DRIVING TO MAKE CONTACT IS AS OUTDATED AS A BUGGY WHIP."

I TOOK THE TIME TO ABSORB ALL SHE'D SAID AND THEN REPLIED WITH, "I WISH I WAS YOU SO I COULD DO ALL THAT, I DO KNOW ENOUGH ABOUT THE CAPABILITES OF COMPUTERS TO UNDERSTAND WHAT YOU'RE SAYING AND TO KNOW YOU'RE RIGHT ABOUT WHAT I HAVE TO DO TO REGAIN A PLACE IN THE FASCINATING WORLD OF ART. PAINTING MY SKYSCAPES BY FIRST PAINTING A WELL INTEGRATED ABSTRACT STRETCHES ME TO MY OUTER LIMITS. I LOVE THAT. I'LL DO WHAT EVER IT TAKES TO NOT BE ANOTHER VICTIM OF THE GREEDY FINANCIAL HIGH FLYERS WHO GOT US INTO THIS MESS. I'LL DO WHAT YOU WOULD DO IF YOU WERE ME, BUT I HAVE A QUESTION FOR YOU: WHEN THE UPTURN OCCURS HOW DO I BREAK INTO GALLERIES THAT SHOW ONLY THE WORK OF THE KNOWN OR FAMOUS ARTISTS AND SELL ONLY TO THE WEALTHY?"

SHE SURPRISED ME BY SAYING, "I OPENED THE SPIRIT GALLERY BECAUSE I *LIKED* JEROME AND FOUND A COMMERCIAL SPACE THAT TO ME WAS AFFORDABLE. I CHOSE ARTISTS BECAUSE I *LIKED* THEIR WORK, NOT BECAUSE I KNEW THEIR ART WOULD *SELL*. I DIDN'T *SELL* ART, IT HAD TO SEDUCE OR CHARM A VIEWER ON ITS OWN. BUT AFTER SEEING A PERSON GO BACK TO A SPECIFIC PAINTING SEVERAL TIMES, I COULD HELP CINCH A SALE BY *SELLING* THE ARTIST, MAKING HIM OR HER EQUALLY IRRESISTIBLE. THAT IS HOW I FUNCTIONED AS AN OWNER-MANAGER OF A LOW-ENDED GALLERY." HOW DO YOU THINK THE OWNER OF A HIGH-END GALLERY OPERATES?"

WANTING TIME TO THINK ABOUT AN ANSWER, I PICKED UP OUR CUPS AND WENT TO "JAKE" FOR ANOTHER REFILL. I WALKED BACK WITH A CUP IN EACH HAND, PUT THEM DOWN, SAT AND SAID, "HIGH-END GALLERY OWNERS, TO ME, MUST BE APPRECIATORS OF THE FINER THINGS, BUT ALSO MUST BE AS MUCH A BOTTOM-LINER AS THE HEAD OF GENERAL MOTORS. THEY MUST ALWAYS DOT I'S AND CROSS T'S AS IN ANY BUSINESS ARRANGEMENT. AT THAT LEVEL, A GALLERY IS PRIMARILY FOR PROFIT. IT IS NOT FILLED WITH ART THE OWNER OR OWNERS *LIKE*. THERE IS ONLY ART THEY *KNOW* WILL *SELL* BECAUSE OF PAST SALES OR AN ARTIST'S REPUTATION. THEY MAY OCCASIONALLY SHOW AN UNKNOWN'S WORK IF THE ARTIST'S BACKROUND IS UNUSUAL AND COMPELLING." I THEN ADDED, "OF COURSE, THERE MUST BE INHERENT VALUE IN THE UNKNOWN'S ART."

ROSEMARIE ASKED, "DO YOU SEE AN INHERENT VALUE IN YOUR SKYSCAPES?"

"DO YOU THINK THE SEVEN PEOPLE WHO BOUGHT MY SKYSCSPES WERE QUALIFIED TO RECOGNIZE THE KIND OF VALUE AN EXPERIENCED DEALER IN ART WOULD SEE? I ENJOY CREATING MY SKYSCAPES. I *LIKE* THEM. I DON'T KNOW AT THIS STAGE IF THEY HAVE A DEEP-ROOTED MEANINGFULNESS."

"I BELIEVE THEY DO, JOHN. YOU'LL HAVE TO BE SATISFIED WITH THAT UNTIL SOMETIME IN THE FUTURE WHEN AN EXCEPTIONALLY ASTUTE UPPER-LEVEL OWNER SETS THE VALUE BY SHOWING AND SELLING THEM."

WE WENT BACK TO THE GALLERY SO SHE COULD DISMANTLE IT PEICE BY PEICE AND I TO LEAVE DETERMINED TO THINK SERIOUSLY ABOUT EVERTHING SHE SAID. I GAVE THE REMAINING SKYSCAPE TO HER TO REMEMBER ME BY.

I NEVER SAW HER OR HEARD FROM ROSEMARIE AGAIN. I DIDN'T HAVE HER HOME PHONE NUMBER AND BECAUSE I WASN'T YET A COMPUTER PERSON I DIDN'T ASK FOR HER E-MAIL ADDRESS. I OFTEN THINK ABOUT HER, WONDERING IF SHE MADE A CONNECTION IN SAN FRANSICO OR HAD TO GO BACK AND FACE ANOTHER CHICAGO WINTER. I MISS HER AND HER "SPIRIT" GALLERY.

 THAT IS NOT AN ACCURATE, WORD FOR WORD RETELLING OF OUR MORNING TOGETHER, BUT THE CORE AND SIGNIFICANCE OF IT I HOPE IS THERE. HER BELIEF IN MY SKYSCAPES AND HER WILLINGNESS TO HELP ME NOT TO GIVE IN TO THE LIMITATIONS OF THE RECESSION WILL NEVER BE FORGOTTEN.

THE FOLLOWING IS AN EXAMPLE OF THE SKYSCAPES THAT SOLD IN ROSEMARIES' SPIRIT GALLERY:

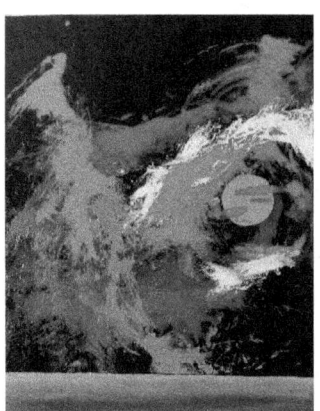

BECAUSE OF ROSEMARIE'S WISE RECOMMENDATIONS, I DID NOT LET THE FINANCIAL DISASTER TURN ME INTO ANOTHER OF ITS VICTIMS. I LET INTUITION AND INSTINCT COVER CANVASES WITH SWIRLING, VIBRANT COLOR THAT EVENTUALLY TURNED INTO FREEWHEELING, FULLY INTEGRATED SKYSCAPES. CREATING EACH ONE BROUGHT AN INORDINATE SENSE OF FULFILLMENT AND THE HOPE THAT MY FANCIFUL SKIES WOULD RENEW MY PILGRIMAGE INTO ART SOMEDAY.

I BOUGHT A COMPUTER, HIRED AN EXCELENT IN-HOME TUTOR, WAS TAUGHT WHAT I NEEDED TO KNOW TO PUT TOGETHER AN ELECTRONIC COLLECTION OF MY SKYSCAPES AND MADE AN INTERNET CONTACT WITH A NUMBER OF THE ONLY GALLERIES STILL ACTIVE, ALL HIGH-ENDED. NOT A SINGLE SKYSCAPE GRACES ONE OF THEIR WALLS.

CHAPTER

28

I WILL SOON HAVE MY NINETY- FIFTH BIRTDAY. I AM GRATEFUL FOR HAVING EACH AND EVERY ONE OF THE NINETY-FOUR PAST BIRTHDAYS THAT TAUGHT ME NOTHING IS FOREVER, NOTHING THAT IS GOOD OR NOTHING THAT IS BAD. FOR ALL OF LIFE, AS WE KNOW IT, THERE HAS ALWAYS BEEN AND ALWAYS WILL BE ENDINGS AND NEW BEGINNINGS.

WHILE LOOKING BACK I'VE SEEN AND STUDIED THE JAGGED, BUT PLEASANT ROUTE MY LIFE HAS TAKEN. I ALSO SEE THAT THE SKEWED, YET INTRIGUIING JOURNEY, IS MOSTLY THE RESULT OF OCCURANCES THAT CHANGED MY LIFE, ALWAYS FOR THE BETTER. LIKE MY MEETING SUE AND ENTHUSIASTICALLY SHARING A LIFE WITH HER FOR OVER FIFTY GLORIOUS YEARS. MY GRADUATING FROM OCS WAS AN EVENT THAT HAD ME TAKING ON A GRAVE RESPONSIBILITY TO COUNTRY, AND BY LIVING UP TO THE LONG-ESTABLISHED IMAGE OF AN OFFICER AND GENTLEMAN CHANGED A YOUNG MAN'S MEANDERING LIFE TO ONE OF PURPOSE. MY INTRODUCING RICKI TO JOAN WEBSTER AT SOCIETY OF MODELS WAS AN EVENT THAT LED TO HER ASTONISHING CAREER. SEEING YOUNG WOMEN PAWING THROUGH RACKS OF RUDI GERNRIEICH'S LAST SEASON'S CLOTHES GAVE ME THE IDEA FOR VANDUSEN GREEN. I LOOK UPON THOSE EVENTS AS GOOD FORTUNE LEADING TO A BETTER MORE PRODUCTIVE LIFE, BUT ONLY BECAUSE IT WAS MY CHOICE TO BE RESOLUTE IN CONTINUING TO EXPLORE WHAT THE CHANGE HAD INTRODUCED. EVEN THOUGH I'M HUMAN WITH AN OVERSIZED CAPACITY FOR CHANGE, I WOULD NOT CHANGE ANY PART OF THE LIFE I'VE HAD.

THE RESILENCE OF THE HUMAN MIND IS OUR STRENGTH. DESPITE OUR EARLY HARDSHIPS AND SHORTCOMINGS, WE HAVE METAMORPHOSED INTO DESIGNERS AND BUILDERS CAPABLE OF CREATING THE INCREDIBLE PYRAMIDS OF EGYPT AND THE MAGNIFICENT CITIES OF ROME, PARIS, NEW YORK AND DUBAI.

CHAPTER

29

I CREDIT OUR ASCENDACY TO TOTAL CONTROL OF OUR PLANET AND EVERY LIVING THING ON IT TO AN EXCLUSIVE DRIVING FORCE, THE FORCE THAT HAS US CONSTANTLY REVISING AND UPGRADING OURSELVES. ALL OF THE OTHER CREATURES THAT EXIST, AND WILL CONTINUE TO EXIST, HAVE ONLY ONE DRIVING IMPULSE, WHICH IS TO SURVIVE.

WE TOO STRIVE TO SURVIVE, BUT WHAT MAKES US INCOMPARABLE IS OUR GREAT AND COMPELLING NEED, EVEN WHEN SECURE, TO STILL MOVE FORWARD, AVOID THE STAID, MAKE CHANGES, SET FRESH GOALS AND LOOK FOR INCENTIVES IN THE LATEST AND NOT THE OLDEST. WE ARE INNATELY DETERMINED TO IMPROVE OUR CONDITIONS AND OUR LIVES. HUMANS HAVE AN UNEQUALIED DRIVE THAT HAS US OVERCOME ANY SEQUENCE OR ARRANGEMENT OF THINGS THAT ARE PROHIBITING PROGRESS, OR THAT ARE DISRUPTIV, OR UNSUITABLE. WE STRIVE FOR A STATE OR CONDITION IN WHICH EVERYTHING FUNCTIONS PROPERLY. UNFORTUNATELY, WE DON'T ALWAYS SUCCEED. WE SHOULD, HOWEVER, BE PROUD OF OUR NEVER HAVING SURRENDERED TO ADVERSITY, BUT HAVE ALWAYS ALLOWED A RESTLESS DESIRE, TO OVERCOME CATASTROPHIES AND LIMITATIONS OF ANY SORT. HERE THEN IS THE MOST CRITICAL, FAR-REACHING, MEANINGFUL AND RELEVANT QUESTION TO MYSELF: WHY HAVE WE YET TO REALIZE THAT OUR RUTHLESS AMBITION TO ACHIEVE, IF PROPERLY FOCUSED, COULD HELP SOLVE OUR LIFE THREATING DISTRACTIONS AND DELEMMAS?

SOME OF US HAVE FOUND LIFE INTOLERABLE WHEN SUFFERING FROM A GROUNDLESS, IRRATIONAL AND UNTENABLE DENIAL OF EQUAL OPPORTUNITIES. WOMEN FOUGHT FOR, AND WON, THE RIGHT TO VOTE, STAND FOR ELECTORIAL OFFICE AND EQUAL CIVIL RIGHTS.

IN THE UNITED STATES, AFTER A CIVIL WAR TO FREE THE SLAVES, THE LIBERATED BLACKS AND THEIR DECENDANTS HAD TO MARCH AND DIE FOR THE RIGHT TO EAT A MEAL AT ANY LUNCH COUNTER OF THEIR CHOICE, OR TO RIDE IN THE FRONT OF THE BUS. THEIR AMENDED RIGHTS TO EQUAL TREATMENT AND EQUAL EMPLOYMENT OPPORTUNITIES WERE ON HOLD SO THEIR NEED FOR BASIC PARITY TURNED INTO A DANGEROUSLY COMBATIVE FORCE DEMANDING FAIRNESS. THOSE WHO DARE TO STAND SHOULDER TO SHOULDER AND FIGHT FOR ACKNOWLEDGEMENT OF THEIR INHERENT VALUE SHOULD BE PRAISED RATHER THAN BEATEN BACK FROM ATTAINING SUCH A SIMPLE BUT WORTHY GOAL. WHY ISN'T OUR WILLINGNESS TO OVERCOME ALL OBSTICALS TO EQUALITY BE WORTHY OF PRAISE INSTEAD OF BILLY CLUBS, SNARLING DOGS AND FIRE HOSES?

TO CLARIFY MY POSITION ON OUR ASCENDENCY TO TOTAL DOMINANCE OF OTHER LIFE, I WILL LIST ONLY A FEW OF OUR ASTONISHING ACCOMPLISHMENTS THAT PROVES OUR COMPENCY. THEY BEGAN THOUSANDS OF YEARS AGO WHEN A VERY EARLY ANCESTOR PICKED UP A LARGE ROCK AND SMASHED

A SMALLER ONE. IT WAS OUR FIRST STEP ALONG THIS ODYSSEY THAT AFFIRMS OUR SINGLENESS AND INNER VALUE.

WHAT BROUGHT US KEEN EDEGED SHARDS THAT SERVED AS TOOLS AND MUCH WELCOMED DEFENSIVE WEAPONS WAS FOR HUMANKIND A MOST IMPORTANT EVENT. THE WEAPON ALLOWED US TO WANDER ABOUT WITH GREATER SAFETY TO FIND THE BEST HUNTING AND GATHERING SPOTS. THE SHARD AS A TOOL ALLOWED US CONSTRUCT CRUDE SHELTERS WHERE THERE WERE NO CAVES. IT WAS A TINY STEP, BUT IT SAVED US FROM BEING NOTHING MORE THAN ANOTHER APE COMPETING TO SURVIVE.

THE SHARD WAS AN AWAKING. OVER TIME, WE DESIGNED AND BUILT MORE EFFICIENT TOOLS AND BUILT MORE DURABLE SHELTERS. OF ALL THE LIVING THINGS WE WERE THE ONLY CONSCIOUS THING CAPABLE OF SUCH INTELLECUAL AND DEXTERIAL FEATS. MUCH LATER WE HUMANS CONCEIVED, AND CONSTRUCTED MULTILAYERED BUILDINGS THAT HOUSED HUNDREDS OF PEOPLE AND THEIR ENTERPRISES. OUR WEAPONS ARE NOW EXTENDED TO ATOM AND HYDROGEN BOMBS CONCEIVED AND BUILT BY DEDICATED HUMANS.

WE TRAVELED FAR AND WIDE EXPLORING, AND GREW WEARY OF LABORIOUSLY WALKING EVERYWHERE. WE CAPTURED AND DOMESTICATED AN ANIMAL WITH FOUR LEGS, SHARP HOOVES, A BIG MOUTH WITH LARGE TEETH AND WEIGHED 900 TO 1100 POUNDS. WE TAUGHT THE HORSE TO FOLLOW OUR COMMANDS AND RODE ON ITS BACK TO WHEREVER WE WANTED TO GO. WE DESIGNED AND BUILT CARRIAGES SO A HORSE COULD TAKE TWO OR THREE OF US SHOPPING AND OUR LADIES TO VIST FRIENDS. THE HORSE WAS HITCHED TO WAGONS AND HAULED GOODS TO AND FROM MARKETS.

THE HORSE, HOWEVER, HAD ITS DRAWBACKS. IT TIRED WHEN ASKED TO GO LONG DISTANCES. IT HAD TO BE FED AND HOUSED. OUR OPPORTUNISTIC FOREFATHERS */63

.+

OMEHOW TRAPPED STEAM AND PUT TOGETHER A POWERFUL STEAM ENGINE, CALLED A LOCOMOTIVE. IT WAS A LARGE WHEELED MACHINE MOVING VEHICLE THAT NEEDED RAILS TO TRAVEL ON. WE WERE UNDETERED. WE LAID MILE UPON MILE OF TRACKS, IMAGINED PASSENGER CARS, SHAPED AND FORMED THEM TO BE PULLED ON THE TRACKS BEHIND THE LOCOMOTIVE. PEOPLE WANTING TO GO TO ANOTHER PLACE HUNDREDS OF MILES AWAY RODE IN RELATIVE COMFORT TO THEIR DESTINATION. EVER ENTERPRISING, WE HUMANS RECOGNIZED POTENTIAL AND FREIGHT CARS APPEARED BEHIND THE LOCOMOTIVES AND MANFACTURES HAD A MEANS TO SHIP THEIR PRODUCTS TO OUTLETS ACROSS STATES AND OVER MOUNTAINS AND AROUND LAKES FASTER AND MORE SAFELY THAN EVER BEFORE.

IMPROVED CONDITONS FOR LONG DISTANCES HAD US THINKING ABOUT REPLACING THE BELOVED HORSE FOR SHORT DISTANCES, SO WE INVENTED THE AUTOMOBILE. ONE OF US, HENRY FORD, STARTED MASS PRODUCING THE MODEL T, AN AFFORDABLE AUTO FOR THE MIDDLE CLASS IN 1908. THE ONLY APPLICABLE COMPARISONS OF THE MODEL T AND TODAY'S SLEEK, POWERFUL CARS ARE THE NECESSARY FOUR WHEELS AND THE MEANS OF LOCOMOTION, AN ENGINE. TIGHTLY ENCLOSED WE RIDE IN FORM FITTING SEATS WITH THE INTERIOR TEMPERATURE AUTOMATICALLY CONTROLLED AT A COMFORTABLE LEVEL IN BOTH THE SUMMER AND WINTER MONTHS.

ENVIOUS OF THE BIRDS, AND NOT TO BE OUTDONE, WE PUT TOGETHER A MOTORIZED, MECHANICAL CONTRIVANCE WITH A FIXED WING THAT COULD OUT PERFORM THE EAGLE. IN MY LIFE TIME, WE HAVE PROGRESSED FROM A ONE ENGINE, OPEN COCKPIT PLANE TO EXTRATERRESTRIAL SPACE SHIPS THAT CAN FLY US TO THE MOON AND LAND ON MARS TO PHOTOGRAPH AND SAMPLE ITS SURFACE, WE CAN BE JET PROPELLED ABOVE THE EARTH TO ANY PLACE ON THIS EARTH IN A MATTER OF HOURS, NOT WEEKS. I FIND THAT KIND OF PROGRESSION HARD TO COMPREHEND, DESPITE MY KNOWING IT FIRST HAND.

I GOT UP THIS MORNING EAGER TO SHOW WHY THIS CREATURE, THAT LOOKED LIKE A REFINED APE, BUILT DWELLING STRUCTURES THAT WERE MUCH MORE THAN A NEST AND TRAVELED TO THE FAR REACHES OF THIS GLOBE ON FOOT, BECAME REMARKABLY CLOSER TO WHAT WE ARE TODAY. EARLY HUMANS BECAME UNRIVALED IN THIS WORLD BY ANSWERING A PRESSING ENCOURAGEMENT TO GO BEYOND GRUNTS AND GRACELESS HAND SIGNALS TO COMMUNICATE. WE, WITHOUT A HELPFUL OTHER WORLDLY RESOURCE, BEGAN TO VOCALIZE WORDS THAT IN THE COURSE OF TIME TURNED A FEW DESCRIPTIVE WORDS INTO A FULL-BLOWN, SPOKEN AND WRITTEN INTERCHANGE.

CURIOUS, I ASKED THE COMPUTER FOR THE NUMBER OF LANGUAGES THERE ARE TODAY AND LEARNED THAT IT WAS DIFFICULT FOR LINQUISTS TO GIVE THE CORRECT ANSWER. THE ETHNOLOGUE ORGANIZATION SAYS 6900. THE LINGUISTIC SOCIETY OF AMERICA SAYS 6800. I WAS STUNNED THAT THERE ARE BETWEEN 6800 AND 6900 DISTINCT SPOKEN LANGUAGES.

COMMON SENSE HAD ME UNDERSTAND THAT WE MAY EACH HAVE A DIFFERENT SET OF FINGER PRINTS, AN INDEPENDENT, UNDUPLICATED DNA, BUT SEPARATE POPULATIONS WITH UNRELATED CULTURES CREATED OVER 6000 DIFFERENT LANGUAGES, AT APPROXIMATELY THE SAME TIME. ALL OF US, DESPITE DIFFERENT BACKGROUNDS, ENVIRONMENTS AND SKIN COLORS, HAVE HADIDENTICAL GOALS.

PUTTING ALL OUR TRIUMPS TOGETHER IS, TO ME, EMPRESSIVE ENOUGH FOR US TO SEE OURSELVS FOR WHAT WE ARE: PHENOMENAL, REMARKAKABLE, SINGULAR, INCOMPARABLE IN OUR SOLAR SYSTEM AND POSSIBLY BEYOND.

THERE IS AN EXCLUSIVE HUMAN NEED TO DEVELOP OURSELVES BY WAY OF GRADUAL ALTERATIONS. THE CONTINUOUS TRANSFORMATIONS ASSIGN US A PURPOSE AND, IN TURN, BRING MEANING TO OUR PRESENCE HERE ON EARTH. SO WHERE WILL THIS INSATIABLE DEMAND TO ADVANCE OURSELVES TAKE US? WILL THE SLOW BUT STEADY MOST MONUMENTAL TRANSFORMATIONS BE THE DIMISSAL OF DEATH? OR WOULD IT BE A FINAL CIVILITY AND EDIFICATION THAT WOULD MAKE OUR WORLDWIDE PRISONS NO LONGER NECESSARY?

WE ARE LIVING IN THE HERE AND NOW, SO WHAT IS IMPORTANT AT THE PRESENT IS TO KNOW THAT WE ARE UNITED AND HAVE A PURPOSE, WHICH IS TO INITIATE A MIRACULOUS TRANSFORMATION FOR THE FUTURE OF HUMANKIND THAT MAY VERY WELL BE OUR HELPING THE WAYWARD AND MISGUIDED FIND THEIR TRUE SELVES.

HUMANKIND IS MARVELOUSLY UNIQUE. WE MUST HONOR OUR INCOMPARABLE NECCESSITY FOR IMPROVEMENT AND PAY HOMAGE TO OURSELVES FOR OUR CONCEIVING AND DEVELOPING THE

MEANS THROUGH WHICH WE CONTINUALLY RESPOND TO SOMETHING REQUIRED. WE HUMAN BEINGS ARE WORTHY OF THE HIGHEST SELF-REGARD FOR OUR VISIONS AND ACCOPLISHMENTS THAT BEGAN BY THE SPLITTING OF A ROCK.

CHAPTER

30

WE SHOULD BE A PERPETUAL AWE OF THE WHOLE OF THE HUMAN RACE. HOW MANY MORE ASTONISHING MIRACLES, LIKE SENDING A SPACE CRAFT TO MARS, CONVERTING GENDERS, AND MASS PRODUCING COMPUTERS MUST WE COMPLETE TO HAVE US ACCEPT JUST HOW INORDINATE, INDEPENDENT AND DESERVING WE ARE OF EVERLASTING RESPECT.

I CHERISH MY GIFT OF LIFE, MY HUMAN INDEPENDENCE AND A PERSONAL NEED TO PRESERVE AND PROTECT EVERY LIVING THING.

PEOPLE HAVE MADE ACCEPTING A HIGHER POWER COMMON TO ALL CULTURES, TO ANSWER QUESTIONS THAT WE DIDN'T HAVE SATISFACTORY ANSWERS. WHEN GOOD AND BAD THINGS HAPPENED, AND WE KNEW THAT WE DIDN'T HAVE THE POWER TO START OR END WHAT HAD OCCURRED.

TODAY, WE HAVE ANSWERES. WE KNOW WHAT CAUSES THINGS TO OCCUR. WE HAVE DONE GOOD JOB OF TAKING CARE OF OURSEVES. IF AT TIMES WE HAVEN'T, IT IS OUR OWN FAULT. I CHERISH MY GIFT OF LIFE WHICH IS FREELY GIVEN WITH NO STRINGS ATTACHED. I WISH NO ONE OR NO ONE THING HARM.

I REGRET MY BEING A SLOW LEARNER, A LATE COMER TO TRUTH., ONLY NOW AS THE LAST OF THE SAND SPILLS DOWN A METAPHORICAL HOUR GLASS AM I ABLE TO SEE THROUGH A CULTURALLY INHERENT MUCK AND MAKE OUT WHAT HAS BEEN OBSCURE FOR SO LONG A TIME. I DON'T LOOK FOR SYMPATHY. I'M TOO THANKFUL THAT I CAN FINALLY SEE WHAT SHOULD HAVE BEEN EVIDENT WHEN THE TOP OF THE GLASS WAS FULL. BUT I MUST ASK, WHY IS COMPREHENDING THE OVERT, THE GLARING OR THE OBVIOUS SO STAGGERINGLY DIFFICULT?

WHY DO SOME OF US SEE OUR WORLD FILLED WITH TOO MANY INTICMENTS? WHY ARE THERE THOSE WHO WISH TO PUNISH THE SINGERS AND DANCERS WHO TAKE AN INNOCENT DELIGHT IN THE FIRST WARM DAY OF SPRING? OR CONDEMN THOSE WHO SEEK A LOVE OF PASSION? OR WANT TO QUIET THE LAUGHTER OF CHILDREN?

THE ATTEMPT TO DENY EARTHLY PLEASURES IS A CONDEMNATION OF THE DENIER. THOSE WHO DISCREDIT OUR WORLD BECOME DANGEROUS. THEIR VIEW OF LIFE MAKES OUR LIVING ON THE PLANET EARTH UNIMPORTANT, AND HUMAN ACHIEVEMENT IRRELEVANT. THE REVOKING OF THE VALUE OF EARHLY LIFE CAN TWIST POVERTY INTO SOMETHING DESIRABLE BECAUSE NOTHING MATTERS. IT CAN TURN LAZINESS INTO A GOOD THING, AND FURNISH THE PASSIVE A JUSTIFICATION FOR FAILURE. IT MAKES THE NEED FOR EDUCATION UNIMPORTANT, AND THEREBY EXCUSES IGNORANCE.

DENYING THE WORLD MAKES FOR SELF-RIGHTEOUSNESS, AND, SADLY, FALSE UPRIGHTEOUSNESS CAN RESULT IN FORGIVING PREJUDICE, BIGOTRY AND INJUSTICE. DENIAL CAN NOURISH INTOLERANCE, SHALLOWNESS AND INDOLENCE. REJECTION OF OUR GLORIOUS GLOBE IS A GLARING DISSERVICE TO HUMANKIND. IT WILL NOT STOP OUR MOVING CONSTANTLY AHEAD, BUT IT CAN CAUSE UNWANTED AND UNEEDED DELAYS,

WE HOMO SAPIENS HAVE BEEN ON THIS EARTH, ACCORDING TO THE ANTHROPOLOGISTS, FOR 35,000 YEARS, WHILE OUR PREDECESSORS WERE AROUND FOR A COUPLE OF MILLION. OUR IMMEDIATE ANCESTORS WERE MORE UPRIGHT, MORE AGILE AND HAD A LARGER BRAIN. THE WEIGHTIER BRAIN PERMITTED THEM TO BE LESS RELIANT ON INSTINCT, MORE SELF-WILLED AND INVENTIVE. FOR THOUSANDS OF YEARS, THEY CHANGED SLOWLY BUT STEADILY. THEY EMERGED BECAUSE THEY WERE ABLE TO ACCUMULATE KNOWLEDGE AND USE IT TO EXPLORE AND INTERPRET. THEY WERE TRULY DIFFERENT FROM THE OTHER ANIMALS DUE TO THEIR ABILITY TO PREFORM AN ACTVITY WE CALL IMAGINING. PERCEIVING MAKES THINGS HAPPEN AND BRINGS ABOUT CHANGES AND THOSE CHANGES GRADUALLY PUT US OUTSIDE NATURE'S DESIRE FOR ORDER. ALL CREATURES BEFORE THE HOMO SAPIENS HAD FOLLOWED PATTERNS THAT WERE FIRMLY ESTABLISHED. PLANTS AND ANIMALS WERE AN INTEGRAL PART OF A SCHEME, CONTRIBUTING MINDLESSLY TO ITS ENDURANCE AND CONTINUATION. IF WE HAD NOT APPEARED, THE WORLD AND ALL LIVING RELATIONSHIPS WOULD HAVE REMAINED THE SAME AS IT WAS 35,000 YEARS AGO, EXCEPT FOR SUDDEN HEAVES AND SHIFTS FROM BELOW THAT WOULD HAVE REARRANGED A PART OF THE EARTH'S SURFACE. WE, THE NEW KIDS IN THE NEIBORHOOD, TURNED THE EARTH AND ITS RESERVE OF RICHES INTO A PLACE THAT WE COULD COMMAND TO SERVE OUR GROWING NEEDS AND ASPIRATIONS.

I AM CONTENT HAVING HAD ORDERLY OPPORTUNITIES TO RESPOND TO EVENTS. OF ALL OF THE INCIDENTS THAT BROUGHT ABOUT THE MOST DEFINING MOMENT, FOR WHICH I'LL ALWAYS BE THE MOST GRATEFUL, IS THE ONE IN A BAR WHERE TWO LADIES, ONE DRUNK, SAT NEXT TO ME AND I MADE AN OFFER TO HELP THE SOBER LADY GET THE DRUNKEN LADY SAFELY HOME.

MY THANKFULNESS FOR THE FIFTY YEARS OF MARRIAGE THAT FOLLOWED THAT OFFER IS BOUNDLESS. I SOMEHOW WON THE FAVOR OF A WOMAN WHO COULD BE REBELLIOUS OR PASSIONATELY LOYAL, RESERVED OR OUTGOING, FEARLESS OR WISELY HESITANT. SHE IS THE MOST COMPLETE PERSON I'VE EVER KNOWN. SUE IS NOW EIGHTY-SEVEN.. HER EYESIGHT IS FAILING AND SHE USES A WALKER, BUT SHE IS STILL THE WOMAN SHE WAS WHEN WE FIRST MET. I LOVE HER DEARLY

WHEN WE HAVE HAD DREAMS AND GOALS REALIZED, WE ARE OF GOOD FORTUNE. IF WE'VE BEEN ABLE TO SHELVE THE IMPAIRMENT OF SELF-DISBELIEF, WE ARE OF GOOD FORTUNE. IF WE HAVE HAD AN EXISTENCE WITH LIFE-CHANGING EVENTS REQUIRING DECISIONS AND OUR EVERY CHOICE LED TO OUR ADVANTAGE, WE MUST ACCEPT THAT GOOD FORTUNE IS UNDENIABLY REAL. IT CAN OVERSEE, SWAY, GOVERN REGULATE OR TAKE CONTROL OVER THE REALITY WE LIVE WITH DAILY. IF YOU HAVE TAKEN A WRONG TURN, GO BACK TO THE EVENT THAT MADE THAT FORK IN THE ROAD AND TAKE THE ONE NOT YET TRAVELED. A DELAYED GOOD FORTUNE MAY STILL BE YOURS TO SAVOUR. WE ARE NOT THE RESULT OF SOME OTHER POWER, BUT ONLY OURSELVES.

CHAPTER

31

MY DAD AND EDITH DIED QUIETLY AND PEACEFULLY A LONG TIME AGO. I BOUGHT THEM A SMALL HOUSE IN PANORAMA CITY, CALIFORNIA. ON DAD'S MINISCULE RAILROAD PENSION, THEY LIVED THERE FINACIALLY SECURE AND HAPPILY FOR TWENTY-SIX YEARS.

RICKI AND I HAVE HAD FEW CONTACTS OVER THE YEARS, BUT ONE NIGHT, ABOUT TEN YEARS AGO, SHE CALLED ME, HERE IN PRESCOTT, TO SAY THAT THE BIGGEST MISTAKE OF HER LIFE WAS DIVORCING ME, THAT EVERYYHING WORTH WHILE THAT HAD HAPPENED TO HER WAS BECAUSE OF ME.

SURPRISED BY HER CALL AND THE COMMENTS, (I DON'T KNOW WHY I'M ALWAYS ALMOST SPEACHLESS WHEN CAUGHT OFF GUARD BY SURPRISING COMMENTS) ALL I COULD THINK TO SAY WAS, "THANK YOU."

SHE WENT ON WITHOUT ACKNOWLEDGING MY RESPONSE, "I THOUGHT WE COULD LIVE SEPERATELY FOR A WHILE AND THEN GET BACK TOGETHER."

THAT, STRUCK ME AS BEING AS ILLOGICAL AS HER TELLING ME, IN A CROWDED RESTAURANT, SHE WANTED A DIVORCE BECAUSE I HAD OUTGROWN HER.

I SAID, "RICKI, YOU DIDN'T ASK FOR A SEPERATION, YOU INSISTED THAT YOU WANTED A DIVORCE. THERE'S A DIFFERENCE."

SHE THEN SAID, "BUT WHY DID YOU GET MARRIED? WHY COULDN'T YOU HAVE STAYED SINGLE FOR A WHILE?" SHE HUNG UP. I SAT DAZED WITH THE PHONE BUZZING IN MY EAR.

I WENT TO BED STILL ASTONISHED BY THE CALL. THE NEXT COUPLE DAYS HELPED ME FIGURE OUT WHAT HAD PROMPTED IT:

I KNEW FROM CONVERSATIONS I'D HAD WITH MY DAUGHTER THAT HER MOTHER HADN'T FARED AS WELL AS A BEAUTIFUL, UNENCUMBERED LADY SHOULD HAVE. AFTER SELLING HER 50% INTEREST IN VANDUSEN GREEN TO HER PARTNER, ARLEN GREENWOOD, SHE WAS WITHOUT IT FORTIFYING HER WITH AN ERSATZ INDEPENDENCE. SHE HAD, UNFORTUNETLY, REVERTED TO THE NEED TO BE TAKEN CARE OF. SHE HAD RELATIONSHIPS, BUT NONE WAS PERMANENT. SHE SAID THAT DIVORCING ME WAS A MISTAKE. TO ME, IT WASN'T A MISTAKE. IT WAS A HEARTLESS MISCALCULATION. SHE IS CURRENTLY

LIVING NEAR OUR DAUGHTER, OUR GRANDCHILDREN AND GREATGRAND CHILDREN IN MOUNT VERNON WASHINGTON.

SOMEBODY HAS PUT TOGETHER EXCELENT WEBSITES THAT GRAFICALLY AND TEXTUALLY TELL OF HER HOLLYWOOD BACKGROUND AND HER HUGE SUCCESS AS A SUPER MODEL.

I AM NOT REFERRED TO IN THE WEBSITES BY NAME, OR SINGLED OUT AS THE FATHER OF HER CHILDEN. ACCORDING TO THE TEXTS I'M A PHANTOM HUSBAND. I UNDERSTAND THAT THE WEBSITES ARE ABOUT HER AND HER CAREER AND SHE DIDN'T NEED TO REFER TO A HUSBAND PAVING THE WAY TO HER CAREER, MAKING CONTROLING DECISIONS AND ORIGINATING AND GUIDING VANDUSEN GREEN.

I DID FIND A REFERENCE TO VANDUSEN GREEN CALLING IT, "ONE OF THE MOST FAMOUS BOUTIQUES IN ENCINO." DOES ENCINO, A SMALL PART OF SANFERNADO VALLEY HAVE A SPECIAL SIGNIFICANCE?

VANDUSEN GREEN WAS MUCH MORE THAN A SMALL SHOP OR "BOUTIQUE." IT WAS A VERY SUCCSSFUL WORKING OUT OF A CONCEPT THAT PRECEEDED THE SAME IDEA BECOMING THE BASIS FOR THE RAPID GROWTH OF FACTORY OUTLET MALLS ACROSS THE COUNTRY. IT WAS ALSO A VERY SUCCESSFUL BRAIN WAVE THAT BECAME AN EVENT THAT PERMENANTLY CHANGED HER LIFE AND MINE.

TO SEE THE WELL EXECUTED BUT INCOMPLETE WEBSITE, LOG INTO RICKI VANDUSEN, SUPER MODEL. IT'S WORTH THE TIME TO BRING IT UP.

RICKI WAS, AND REMAINS, AN ENIGMA THAT IS HARD TO DISENTANGLE. I WISH THAT SOMEONE HAD MADE POSSIBLE A MEANINGFUL, LASTING RELATIONSHIP. I'M SORRY SHE'S ALONE.

MY SON, STEPHEN, AFTER NOW FIVE MARRIAGES AND FOUR LEGAL TERMENATIONS AND A READY DISMISSAL OF THE KIDS HE SIRED, IS SEVENTY YEARS OLD AND STILL AS HANDSOME AS HE WAS WHEN PITCHING FOR THE AIR FORCE'S BASEBALL TEAM IN EUROPE. WE DO NOT STAY IN TOUCH.

DARRAGH NEVER DID DO ANYTHING WITH HER ART OR HER BACHELOR DEGREE ALLOWTNG HER TO TREAT AND HELP TROUBLED TEENAGERS. SHE MARRIED AND RAISED FOUR GREAT KIDS WHO NOW HAVE CHILDREN OF THEIR OWN. SHE LIVES IN MOUNT VERNON, WASHINGTON.

LOOKING BACK AS THROUGHLY AS I HAVE, I MUST NOT FAIL TO INCLUDE MY MOTHER IN THIS EXERCISE OF REMEMBERENCES. I RECALL ONLY ONE INSTANCE WHEN SHE WAS A CARING MOTHER OR FRIEND. DO I REGRET NOT GETTING WARM HUGS OR REASSURANCES WHEN I NEEDED THEM LIKE ANY CHILD? NO, BECAUSE IN IOWA I WAS A PART OF A FAMILY MADE UP OF LOTS OF UNCLES, AUNTS AND COUSINS. MY INCLUSION IN THEIR SPONTANIOUS INTERCHANGES OF TAUNTS AND HIGH SPIRITED ACTIVITIES PARTLY MADE UP FOR MY MOTHER'S LACK OF ATTENTION AT HOME. I BELIEVE THAT THEY AND MY FATHER UNKNOWINGLY CREATED SURROUNDINGS OF NORMALCY.

I REMEMBER CLEARLY THAT I WAS FREE TO WALK INTO ANY RELATIVES' HOME - FRONT DOORS WERE NEVER LOCKED, THAT PHONES HUNG ON THE WALL AND A FRIENDLY OPERATER ANSWERED WHEN IT WAS CRANKED.

PLAYING HIDE-AND-SEEK WITH MY COUSINS WAS A MOST POPULAR SUMMER GAME, CATCHING LIGHTING BUGS IN A JAR WAS A CLOSE SECOND. TOGETHER, WE YEARNED FOR THE JAW BREAKERS AND PENNY CANDY IN THE GROCERY STORES' GLASS CASES AND THE PICKLES THAT WERE IN OPEN BARRELS TO MAKE OUR MOUTHS WATER.

PROUDLY SHOWING OFF NEW CLOTHES ON EASTER WAS SO VERY SPECIAL. CHRISTMAS EVE, WITH GRANDPA HANDING OUT THE PRSENTS TO THE FAMILY FROM UNDER A TINSLE LADEN TREE, WAS THE EVENT OF THE YEAR,

ADULTS EATING AT ONE TABLE AND CHILDREN AT ANOTHER ESTABLISHED AN EARLY FREEDOM AND INDEPENDENCE AND BROUGHT A PEACEFUL SILENCE TO THE ADULTS.

GRANDMA PUTTING A TOWEL OVER HER KNEADED DOUGH AND LETTING IT SIT TO RISE OVER NIGHT TO BE READY FOR BREAKFAST WAS A COMMON SIGHT.

EVERY THING WE THOUGHT AND DID WAS SHARED WITH OTHERS. WE HUDDLED SILENTLY AROUND A CRYSTAL RADIO, WITH A CAR LOADED WE WENT FOR DRIVES IN THE COUNTRY ON SUNDAY AND WE GATHERED TOGETHER AT THE RALROAD DEPOT TO WATCH THE TRAINS PULL IN.

THIS SIMPLE SHARING GAVE ME A BASIS THAT HELPED ME ACCEPT HER LEAVING US AS SHE DID IN CHICAGO. WITHOUT IT, MY MOTHER'S HATEFUL INFLUENCES MAY HAVE .CUT DEEPER INTO MY PSYCHE. I AM GRATEFUL FOR THE WARMTH OF SHARING IN AN INNOCENT, UNCOMPLICATED TIME.

I'M NOT ANXIOUSLY AWAITING THE LAST POSSIBLE LIFE-CHANGING EVENT, BUT I'LL ACCEPT IT, HOPEFULLY, AS NATURALLY AS I HAVE ALL OF THE OTHER LIFE-CHANGING ONES.

A FRIEND TOLD ME THAT I SHOULD PAINT A SELF-PORTRAIT TO LEARN ABOUT MYSELF. I DID, BUT DIDN'T LEARN A DAMN THING. I HAVE LEARNED MORE ABOUT MYSELF WHILE DIGGING INTO MY NINETY-FIVE YEARS THAN I NEED TO KNOW TO GET TO NINETY-SIX, BUT IT WAS NOT A WASTE OF PRECIOUS TIME. I THOROUGHLY ENJOYED WRITING "LOOKING BACK." IT KEPT ME BUSY AND I APPRECIATE THAT.

JOHN HINSEY, 9/13/2016

www.ingramcontent.com/pod-product-compliance
Lightning Source LLC
Chambersburg PA
CBHW051948280526
45789CB00009B/3218

9781539146834